THE EGG COOKBOOK

D1361262

THE EGG COOK BOOK

The Creative Farm-to-Table
Guide to Cooking Fresh Eggs

 HEALDSBURG PRESS

Copyright © 2014 by Healdsburg Press, Berkeley, California

No part of this publication may be reproduced, stored in a retrieval system or transmitted in any form or by any means, electronic, mechanical, photocopying, recording, scanning or otherwise, except as permitted under Section 107 or 108 of the 1976 United States Copyright Act, without the prior written permission of the publisher. Requests to the publisher for permission should be addressed to the Permissions Department, Healdsburg Press, 918 Parker St., Suite A-12, Berkeley, CA 94710.

Limit of Liability/Disclaimer of Warranty: The publisher and the author make no representations or warranties with respect to the accuracy or completeness of the contents of this work and specifically disclaim all warranties, including without limitation warranties of fitness for a particular purpose. No warranty may be created or extended by sales or promotional materials. The advice and strategies contained herein may not be suitable for every situation. This work is sold with the understanding that the publisher is not engaged in rendering medical, legal or other professional advice or services. If professional assistance is required, the services of a competent professional person should be sought. Neither the publisher nor the author shall be liable for damages arising herefrom. The fact that an individual, organization or website is referred to in this work as a citation and/or potential source of further information does not mean that the author or the publisher endorses the information the individual, organization or website may provide or recommendations they/it may make. Further, readers should be aware that Internet websites listed in this work may have changed or disappeared between when this work was written and when it is read.

For general information on our other products and services or to obtain technical support, please contact our Customer Care Department within the United States at (866) 744-2665, or outside the United States at (510) 253-0500.

Healdsburg Press publishes its books in a variety of electronic and print formats. Some content that appears in print may not be available in electronic books, and vice versa.

TRADEMARKS: Healdsburg Press and the Healdsburg Press logo are trademarks or registered trademarks of Callisto Media Inc. and/or its affiliates, in the United States and other countries, and may not be used without written permission. All other trademarks are the property of their respective owners. Healdsburg Press is not associated with any product or vendor mentioned in this book.

ISBN: Print 978-1-62315-388-5 | eBook 978-1-62315-389-2

Contents

Appendixes

Introduction

There is a good chance that at some point in the last week you ate an egg in some form. Perhaps it was for breakfast, on a sandwich, or in a cake or cookie for dessert. Eggs are a huge part of most meal plans and many people are taking a special interest in this amazing food. Many consumers want new recipes, cooking techniques, and even information on how to raise their own chickens in order to have access to healthy, fresh eggs daily. This book will answer many questions you might have concerning eggs (and chickens) as well as provide more than 110 easy recipes to expand your cooking repertoire and introduce new ways to enjoy eggs.

This book is broken down into easy-to-follow sections that:

- Introduce various chicken breeds
- Educate about the types of eggs available
- Answer common questions on raising chickens and cooking with eggs
- Describe egg dishes from around the world
- Walk you through basic egg preparations
- Discuss the tools and equipment that make egg cooking and preparation simpler
- Outline tips to save time and money when planning, preparing, and storing your egg-based meals

Eggs are some of the most economical ingredients for home-cooked meals, which have become increasingly important for people looking to scale back on dining out and avoid processed, pre-made foods and meals. Backyard chicken coops take home meal preparation one step further, making fresh, nutritious eggs readily available for those carefully considering health and budget. You certainly don't need to set up your own chicken coop if you want to include more eggs in your diet, but it is nice to know that so much support and information is available if you wish to go this route. Bottom line, eggs are a healthy, versatile meal choice, and they are quick and easy to prepare for both beginners as well as seasoned home cooks.

CHAPTER ONE

The Chickens and the Eggs

Eggs probably seem like the simplest ingredients in your fridge, but there is a great deal more to this humble food than you might think. For one, there are many types of eggs from many types of chickens from which to choose.

Whether scouring the supermarket shelves or picking up a dozen eggs at your local farmers' market, you might be confused by the different packaging labels and varieties of eggs available. Eggs can be labeled as organic, omega-3 enhanced, free-range, vegetarian, cage-free, humane, or pastured. These varieties of eggs are actually describing the conditions in which the hens live when producing the eggs, rather than anything that happens to the egg itself. In the interest of sourcing healthier product, it is important to be aware of where your eggs came from (i.e., how the chicken was raised) before you whisk them up into an omelet. See "Not All Eggs Are Equal" below for a more detailed explanation about labels.

If you have the space, permission, and the inclination, consider raising a few chickens to gather your eggs directly from the source. Note that some cities and states have restrictions on home chicken coops. Chickens are incredible birds with unique, quirky personalities that vary depending on the breed. You can have affectionate birds who follow you around like dogs or ones that have silky fur-like feathers and will actually play with your children. Each breed has different strengths and produces different types of eggs, even pretty sky-blue and green ones!

Surprisingly, many people raise chickens in their backyards through the use of mobile coops and enjoy fresh, healthy eggs every day. There is a great deal of information, guidance, and resources available for anyone wanting to try to raise chickens, and it is not as complicated or expensive as you might think. Learning about chickens and eggs will give you a greater appreciation for the fluffy scrambled eggs on your plate.

NOT ALL EGGS ARE EQUAL

The life of an egg before it arrives in your refrigerator can be just as essential as what transpires on the stove top. Unless you are raising your own chickens, it is important to understand the variety of eggs for sale and their differences. Use the Egg Feedback Chart on page 194 to keep track of what eggs best suit your needs.

Store-Bought Conventional Eggs

These are the least expensive eggs most commonly purchased at the supermarket, usually sold in foam containers. Unless labeled otherwise, they come from hens often living in overcrowded cages and in buildings that might never let in the light of day. These hens are fed grains supplemented with vitamins and minerals, and the chickens are usually treated with a daily dose of antibiotics to prevent infection. Conventional eggs are considered a quality protein source as a healthy meat alternative and do contain vitamin A, potassium, and B vitamins such as folic acid, choline, and biotin. However, critics point to the presence of antibiotics as potentially problematic for our health and suggest that poor raising conditions can actually decrease the vitamin and mineral quality of the eggs.

Cage-Free Eggs

Many people have a rosy vision of "cage-free" and "free-range" chickens because these indicate chickens were not raised in cages. Unfortunately, many cage-free environments are still very crowded and dirty, which can stress out the hens and even cause them to injure one another. Some smaller egg producers provide cleaner, less crowded, cage-free hen houses where hens can usually walk around the coop, roost, and lay their eggs in nesting boxes. Cage-free eggs do not necessarily indicate a superior taste or nutritional value compared to confined birds, but many swear by the rich, enhanced taste and higher level of omega-3 fatty acids found in pastured and many farmers' market eggs.

Free-Range Eggs

Free-range eggs come from chickens that have access to the outdoors. This does not mean they can roam freely in a prairie or meadow, although some farmers do raise their poultry this way (in that case, they are "pastured"). Free-range more commonly means the chickens were raised in huge, climate-controlled buildings with daily access to a small portion of the outdoors through a small window or door. However, this does not mean the hens will or can actually venture outdoors. Free-range eggs are more expensive because of the increased overhead costs of the buildings and climate-control technology, but these eggs do not necessarily have a superior nutritional value or taste than those from hens raised completely indoors.

Pasture-Raised or Pastured Eggs

If you like the vision of chickens wandering around the grass able to forage, scratch, take dust baths, socialize, and roost, then pasture-raised eggs are the product you want to purchase. Pasture-raised eggs come from chickens that spend most of their day rambling around in the woods or fields, eating grass, bugs, insects, and other things they can forage. They retreat to the hen house at night for shelter. These eggs come from small egg producers and farmers, and many say they have a richer taste compared to commercially produced eggs because of the hens' natural diet. Pasture-raised eggs are also shown to have less cholesterol, double the vitamin E, and twice the omega-3 fatty acids than standard, commercially produced eggs. The price of these eggs, commonly found at farmers' markets and in some specialty grocery and health food stores, is set by the individual farmer.

Omega-3-Enriched Eggs

These eggs come from hens that are fed a diet high in flaxseed oil, kelp, and other ingredients very rich in omega-3 fatty acids, which transfer to the yolk of the eggs. Since eating foods rich in omega-3 fatty acids can reduce the risk of heart disease, these eggs are meant to support a healthy lifestyle. The controversy of omega-3-enriched eggs comes from the fact that egg yolks also contain some cholesterol that, if eaten in excess, could potentially contribute to heart disease. Note that these eggs tend to be more expensive than other types.

Organic Eggs

These eggs come from chickens that are not fed anything grown using herbicides, pesticides, irradiation, sewage sludge, genetic modifications, or fertilizers. These chickens are not treated with antibiotics or steroids and need to be allowed access to an area that has natural vegetation. The amount of time or access the chickens get to the vegetation is not regulated, so these chickens could live under very similar conditions to factory-raised chickens. Look for some type of seal or certification on the carton to ensure you are getting an organic egg product. Organic feed ingredients have higher production costs, which in turn makes organic eggs more costly. Organic eggs are not necessarily more nutritious than regular eggs, but many people feel better eating eggs that are not contaminated with chemicals or additives. Some say organic eggs, which often have paler yellow yolks, taste better than regular eggs, and this could be due to the chicken's more natural diet.

The common perception that organic eggs are healthier is not entirely true. The nutritional profile of eggs is entirely based on what the chickens are fed, not on whether they are raised in cages or if the feed is treated with pesticides. That is why pasture-raised birds that are allowed to forage for seeds, insects, and other food sources are found to be tastier than other eggs and have higher levels heart-healthy fatty acids.

Vegetarian-Fed Eggs

This is a label you will see quite often in the grocery store. Chickens naturally eat a very eclectic diet and will even eat chicken and eggs if that is what they are fed. Some larger-scale producers have been found to feed their birds meat, fish, chicken, and meat by-products. Vegetarian-fed birds are not fed these products and people are usually willing to pay more for eggs labeled this way. What most people don't realize is that pastured eggs, found to be some of the tastiest, healthiest eggs available, are actually not vegetarian-fed because the foraging chickens often eat seeds, worms, insects, and even frogs, small snakes, and mice if they can catch them. The benefit of the "vegetarian feed" for more industrial eggs, however, ensures that the chicken did not eat any cow, pig, or other chicken matter.

Fertile Eggs

This type of egg has been fertilized by a rooster and will produce a chick if placed in an incubator or if the mother hen sits on it. Fertile eggs are more expensive because production costs are higher and they spoil faster. These eggs are not more nutritious or tastier than regular unfertilized eggs, but some people like them and they are a product sold in many supermarkets.

Pasteurized Eggs

Though similar sounding in name, these eggs should not be confused with pasture-raised eggs. Pasteurized eggs mean that they have been heated to 160°F to destroy potentially harmful bacteria. Many chefs and home cooks buy these eggs so they can be used raw in recipes such as Caesar salad or cookie dough with no risk of salmonella. Pasteurized eggs are stamped with either a "P" or other certification to indicate they have gone through this heating process. These eggs are thought to be no different from other eggs in nutritional value but some say they have a slightly different, more neutral taste when cooked.

Don't call me a chicken

Chicken is a generic label used to describe both males and females of this poultry family, but there are more specific terms that are used when looking at chickens.

- Bantam: a breed of chicken that is about one-third the size of standard chickens.
- Biddy: baby chickens or chicks.
- Chick: a newly hatched baby chicken or very young chicken.
- Cockerel: a male chicken under one year of age.
- Hen: a female chicken at least one year of age.
- Pullet: Chickens less than one year of age.
- Rooster: a male chicken at least one year of age.

BIRDS OF DIFFERENT FEATHERS

It can be very overwhelming to choose your chickens after deciding to try your hand at producing eggs in your backyard. Each type of chicken has a different personality, produces different-colored eggs, and in some cases certain chickens can't survive well in cold weather. Do your research and choose carefully so that your egg-producing experience is successful and fun!

- **Ameraucana** (medium light-blue eggs): These are relatively rare, large birds that can be black, blue, brown red, buff, silver, and white. They were bred originally from Araucana chickens but do not have tufts or the same gene issues. They have a small pea comb as well as fluffy-looking beards and are very winter-hardy. Ameraucanas have fun, friendly personalities in groups but individual birds can be dominant. They are good layers and can produce up to three blue eggs per week.
- **Araucana** (medium blue eggs): These are very rare, pretty small chickens that are rumpless (no tail) and carry a tufted gene that can cause productivity issues (many chicks die in their shells). As a result, although they are hardy and have a friendly personality, they are not the best choice for novice chicken raisers. If you do choose to raise this bird, source your Araucanas from a reputable provider to avoid inbreeding issues. Araucanas are good layers and produce up to three pretty blue eggs per week.
- **Australorp** (large brown eggs): These shiny, black birds have a unique green sheen to their feathers and were developed in Australia from black Orpingtons. Like their ancestors, they have a similar sweet, quiet, and docile temperament. Australorp chickens are very hardy birds suited to cold or hot weather. They are excellent layers, producing about five or more eggs per week.

Ever wonder why some eggs are white while others are brown? In most cases, the color of a chicken's ear lobes will indicate what color eggs they will lay. Chickens with white ear lobes lay white eggs, but there are a couple exceptions, such as chickens with red ear lobes, which lay brown eggs.

- **Buff Orpington** (large brown eggs): An English breed originating in Orpington in the late 1800s, this sweet, pretty bird most commonly has a buff color but can also be black, white, and blue. In mixed flocks, they are often picked on by other birds because of their docile nature, but they are a popular choice for backyard coops because of their cold-weather hardiness. Orpingtons are good layers, producing three to four eggs per week.
- **Cochin** (medium brown eggs): These birds resemble very large, fluffy balls with pretty feathers and are more valued for their sweet nature than their laying ability. They come in a broad range of colors, such as black, buff, white, barred, mottled, birchen, and blue, with fabulous feathered legs. This Asian breed is winter-hardy and can be handled easily. They lay about two eggs per week but are fabulous mothers if you want to raise chicks.
- **Faverolles** (medium light brown or cream eggs): A very popular breed because of their sweet, docile personality and odd but endearing appearance, these French birds are large with fluffy, bearded faces, snowy muffs, and feathered feet. They are hardy in the winter as adults and tend to fall to the bottom of the pecking order in mixed flocks. Faverolles are good layers, averaging about four eggs per week.

- **Leghorn** (extra-large or large white eggs): These medium-size, friendly white birds with large red combs are probably best known from Bugs Bunny cartoons as the Foghorn Leghorn character. They are very winter-hardy but do require a layer of petroleum jelly applied to their combs to prevent frostbite. Leghorn chickens produce four or more extra-large white eggs per week. Some non-white Leghorns produce about three large eggs per week.

- **Plymouth Rock** (large brown eggs): Plymouth Rock chickens were originally introduced as a breed in England in the late 1800s but are now considered more of an American breed. Some varieties of these birds include barred, white, buff, blue, partridge, and silver-stenciled. They have a characteristic bright red face and red earlobes. They are intelligent and friendly but can be very bossy toward other chickens. They are good layers, producing four to five eggs per week, and are very hardy in colder weather.

- **Rhode Island** (extra-large brown eggs): These large red and white birds are so highly regarded that they are the official state bird of Rhode Island. They are a wonderful choice if you are not sure what bird will do well in your climate because they are extremely hardy. Rhode Island chickens can be red or white and have generally easygoing personalities without being broody. They are excellent layers, producing five or more eggs per week.

- **Silkie** (medium white to light-brown eggs): Silkies get their name from their silky feathers that look almost like fur because they lack the tiny cartilage hooks found in feathers. They are originally from China and are documented in historical records dating as far back as the 1500s. Silkies are wonderful pets if you are looking for chickens with docile, gentle personalities. They are also very broody, which makes them less prolific layers than other breeds, and they usually do not lay through the winter. At peak egg production, they can lay one egg per day but not over a consistent or extended period of time.

- **Welsummer** (large chocolate or speckled eggs): The rooster on the Kellogg's Corn Flakes box is probably the most recognized Welsummer bird. These gorgeous chickens originate from Holland and are fabulous foragers but don't mind being in runs either. Unlike many other chicken breeds, Welsummer chickens can be sorted into male and female as chicks quite easily because the females have darker back and head markings. They are very good layers, producing four or more eggs per week, except in the winter, when they lay fewer eggs.

- **Wyandotte** (large pale-brown or tan eggs): These birds are a favorite of farmers and backyard chicken enthusiasts everywhere because they are such reliable layers. Wyandottes are beautiful, heavy birds with decorative feature patterns and rose-colored combs. Wyandotte chickens come in many different varieties, such as silver-laced, golden-laced, white, black, Columbian blue, and barred. They are winter-hardy and usually quite easygoing but have dominant tendencies. They are excellent layers, consistently producing four or more eggs per week.

If you are looking to enjoy an assortment of egg colors for your table or for selling, you can mix and match the following chickens, taking into account personality and geographic limitations:

KNOW YOUR EGG COLORS

Egg Color	Chicken
Blue eggs	Araucanas, Ameraucanas
Blue-green eggs	Araucanas, Ameraucanas
Cream eggs	Polish, Sussexes, Faverolles
Dark chocolate-brown, rust, or red eggs	Barnevelders, Marans, Sexlink, Welsummer
Light blue eggs	Ameraucanas
Light green eggs	Ameraucanas
Light pink eggs	Ameraucanas
Pale brown or tan eggs	Wyandotte
Pink brown eggs	Plymouth Rocks, Salmon Faverolles

Q & A FOR RAISING CHICKENS

Here are some answers to common questions about raising chickens, but by no means is this all of the information you need to know when making this type of lifestyle commitment. Make sure you investigate books and Internet sites and talk to people or farmers who own chickens to get a detailed picture about what is involved with regards to raising chickens.

Is it legal to raise chickens?
This depends on where you live, so before venturing into chicken ownership, check your local bylaws, health codes, and ordinances. Some areas will allow only a set number of birds under very strict guidelines, and other places forbid this practice altogether.

How much will I pay for a chicken?
Cost can depend on the breed, age, and sex of the chicken. Rare breeds and females will cost more. Prices for baby chicks, according to BackyardChicken.com, can range from $1 to $5, while young laying hens can cost between $15 and $25.

Will owning chickens save money?

Most people don't raise their own chickens to save money, but rather to eat a healthier, fresher product. If you have a few chickens for your own egg consumption, you will probably break even or end up slightly out of pocket. If you have a larger number of birds and sell the eggs after considering local laws governing this activity, you might make some money.

Where should I get my chickens?

Always get your birds from reputable farms and hatcheries that you have visited, if possible. Avoid buying only one chicken, even as a pet, because these birds are very social and are not happy when alone.

Is a chicken coop right for me?

If you have decided to raise chickens, think about what type of shelter you need for your birds. Part of this decision depends on whether you get adult birds or want to start your chicken dynasty from chicks. Keep in mind, it can be difficult to tell if your chicks are male or female, so you might end up with less eggs than you want if you get your birds young. You don't need to be fancy with baby chicks as long as you regulate the temperature of their environment with a heat lamp set between 70°F and 90°F, depending on their age. You can actually keep your chicks in a plain, sturdy cardboard box lined with pine shavings for the first few months. Keep a constantly filled water bowl and food dish in the box, and your chicks will be fine.

Once your chicks are older than about two months, you will need to move them to an outdoor coop, as long as it is not during the middle of winter. That is why the best time to get your chicks is the spring, so they can grow in warmer weather. You can find great coops online, so do some research with your budget and the number of chickens you want to raise in mind. A 4-by-8-foot coop is usually large enough for about five chickens to have some space to run and roost, and it should be wrapped completely in wire mesh with holes no bigger than one inch to keep out predators. The coop should protect your chickens from the elements and have nesting boxes (usually 12 inches tall by 12 inches wide by 12 inches long) with straw or wood shavings. Make sure your hens don't sleep in their nests by blocking the nests off at night with pieces of wood or another method. If you provide enough roost space, your birds won't sleep in the nests and dirty them with droppings. Always provide a higher, well-ventilated area in the coop for your chickens to roost.

Some of the best coops can be purchased as kits and are actually mobile (on wheels) so that you can move them around your yard to allow new grass to grow and prevent bare-stripped, muddy areas that can be unhealthy for your birds.

What do chickens eat?

This depends on the age of the bird, but chickens are very skilled predators when it comes to catching insects and worms. Baby chicks can be fed commercial feed or even oats and finely chopped vegetables. You should also mix some sand, gravel, or crushed oyster shells in with the feed. Chickens need grit in their gizzards to help them grind up and digest their food.

When you are feeding your chickens, keep in mind whatever you give them will transfer to the eggs. Chickens can be fed commercial feed or corn but will also eat kitchen scraps of any kind, including chicken! Chickens will eat pretty much anything, but make sure their feed is not moldy or wet, which can also cause health issues.

Along with proper food, you will need to provide adequate water in large buckets and have a heated watering system in the winter.

How often do hens lay eggs?

The entire egg process takes about twenty-five hours from ovulation to laying, and then the process begins again. Several factors can influence the timing, however. Some chicken breeds are more prolific than others, so they are bred specifically for laying eggs. Other breeds are used primarily for meat, so they may not lay as many eggs. Hens lay more eggs in the summer than in the winter, and younger birds between six and twelve months of age lay the most eggs.

How do you collect eggs?

If you have several young chickens, you might be able to collect eggs twice daily. Start by collecting the eggs that have not been sat on by hens, and then carefully lift the birds in their nesting boxes to get the eggs underneath. If your coop is clean, the eggs should also be clean when you pick them up. Eggs have a natural antibacterial coating on them called the bloom, which you should not wash off because this can make the eggs more susceptible to bacteria. If you do choose to clean your eggs, use a dry brush or sanitized cleaning pad. If you need to wash the eggs more thoroughly because of adhered dirt or dried yolk from another broken egg, use water that is slighter warmer than the egg. Cold water will shrink the inside of the egg, which can also lead to bacteria growth. Air dry the wet eggs on a towel. Do not wash your eggs unless they are very dirty.

What makes eggs white or brown?

The type or breed of chicken determines the shell color. White chickens lay white eggs and brown chickens lay brown eggs. There is a misconception about brown eggs being healthier than white eggs. The color of the egg does not determine its nutritional impact. The health of the chicken does, whether it is white or brown.

How are double yolks formed?

Double yolks usually occur in young chickens with immature reproductive systems or in older chickens nearing the end of their egg-producing cycle. These chickens will release two yolks into the same shell.

Do you need a rooster for chickens to lay eggs?

No. Hens lay eggs whether there are roosters around or not. Without roosters, however, these eggs will not be fertilized or grow into chicks. If you do have a rooster, there is a chance the eggs will end up fertilized.

Are chickens noisy?

If you keep hens, you will only really hear them when they feel or are threatened, and when they lay eggs. Roosters, however, can be ear-splitting because they crow all day long, not just in the morning.

Are chickens big?

This will depend on the breed of the chicken and the gender. Roosters are bigger than hens. An average chicken weighs between 4 and 8 pounds.

If you are a novice backyard chicken farmer, you might want to get your chickens as baby chicks rather than trying to incubate them yourself. Doing so requires an incubator and careful temperature and humidity control, which can be tricky. If you get fertilized eggs, you will not know if you are getting hens or roosters, and the eggs will not be vaccinated against two very common and harmful chicken diseases: Marek's disease and coccidiosis.

How old do chickens get?

It is not unusual for chickens to live until eight or ten years of age, but keep in mind that after one year of age, your chickens will decline in egg production little by little each year. Since a healthy, young bird produces one egg per day, your flock will still produce many eggs in total even as they get older.

Why do eggs sometimes have darker yolks?

The color of the egg yolk is determined by what the hen eats. A wheat-based diet will produce light yellow yolks, while a corn- or alfalfa-based diet will produce darker yellow yolks.

How are egg sizes determined?

The weight of individual eggs determines what size they will be labeled as in the store or market. There is a range, however. Some eggs in the same carton will appear to be different sizes, though they have similar weights. The following are common egg size and weight classifications:

- Peewee: 15 ounces
- Small: 18 ounces
- Medium: 21 ounces
- Large: 24 ounces
- Extra-Large: 27 ounces
- Jumbo: 30 ounces

How much work is it to keep chickens?

Chickens are pretty low-maintenance but do require some care on a daily basis.

- **Daily:** Check for eggs and gather what is available, let the chickens in and out of the coop (depending on your setup), and pay attention to proper feeding and watering.
- **Weekly:** If your coop is mobile, move it around to prevent stripping the grass on your property and to allow new grass to grow. If it is stationary, make sure the ground is not too muddy and torn up so the birds can get some exercise.
- **Monthly:** Clean the chicken waste out of the coop and change all the bedding. Check your hens for mites and lice as well because this can cause the birds to become sick.
- **Biannually:** Completely clean and disinfect the coop.

CHAPTER TWO

Cooking with Eggs

Eggs are an ingredient used in almost every culture in the world in a variety of delicious dishes. Eggs are so versatile, they can be whipped to fluffy peaks, baked, fried, transformed into luscious custards, poached, and combined with a vast array of other ingredients, producing wonderfully tasty results.

There are many tools available to help create egg dishes and make the cooking process simpler. You can use a simple skillet, spatula, or saucepan to cook the eggs, but if you want to take egg preparation one step further, consider investing in a few special culinary pieces like ramekins and a crêpe pan.

Once you master the various techniques and have an assortment of tools for cooking eggs, try creating other egg-based dishes from around of the world with the recipes found in this book. Eggs can be very forgiving, so do some experimenting to discover new family favorites.

BASIC TOOLS AND UTENSILS FOR COOKING AND BAKING WITH EGGS

Because eggs are a very popular staple ingredient, there are many utensils and types of equipment specifically designed for cooking and preparing the beloved food. You can certainly prepare eggs with regular pots, bowls, a whisk, and a skillet, but these gadgets can make creating dishes like custards and soufflés easier. Keep your budget and kitchen space in mind when expanding your kitchen tools repertoire. These are some tools to consider when preparing egg recipes:

- **Bowls:** An assortment of glass and stainless steel bowls will meet all your mixing, whipping, and beating needs. Plastic bowls are not as good a choice for beating egg whites in particular because the bowls can absorb fat and heat and inhibit the egg whites from developing into stiff peaks.
- **Cast-Iron Skillet:** This heavy-duty skillet is a perfect tool for frittatas because it can be used both on the stove and in the oven. Make sure to adequately season the skillet using the manufacturer's instructions. After using the skillet, do not to wash it with soap, steel wool, or a coarse sponge because it can scratch and damage the finish.
- **Egg Cooker:** This handy piece of equipment can be used to create omelets, fried eggs, scrambled eggs, hard-boiled eggs, and soft-boiled eggs. It can also steam the eggs in their shells.
- **Egg Cups:** These dainty cups are for serving soft boiled eggs.

- **Egg Piercer:** This special gadget punches a tiny hole in the shell to allow air to escape and help prevent cracking during hard-boiling. It can also make peeling easier. A sterilized pin or needle works just as well.
- **Egg Poacher:** This convenient device can hold either one egg or several eggs with a rack when placed in simmering water.
- **Egg Ring:** This metal ring is meant to hold an egg intact while it is being poached or fried. Look for egg rings with handles for the most convenience.
- **Egg Separator:** This device has a cup to catch the egg yolk and slots to allow the egg whites to slip through. Egg separators can be plastic or metal.
- **Egg Slicer:** With this gadget, it's easy to create perfectly even slices. Simply place the hard-boiled egg in the tray and lower the cutting handle. The parallel wires cut the egg into thin slices. Use the egg slicer to chop the egg too by turning the egg carefully after being sliced and slicing it again lengthwise.
- **Egg Timer:** An egg timer can be as simple as an hourglass to measure the correct time for perfect soft-boiled eggs or as advanced as a device with a digital readout to boil, poach, and bake eggs to perfection.
- **Handheld Electric Mixers and Egg Beaters:** Electric mixers are very useful for beating egg whites to stiff peaks, but rotary-style egg beaters can be an equally effective a tool at a much lower cost, if you're willing to put in some muscle power.
- **Kitchen Torch:** If you enjoy making the classic, egg-based custard crème brûlée, a small kitchen blowtorch helps create a crunchy, caramelized crust.
- **Omelet Pan:** These pas are shallow skillets specifically designed for making omelets. They can range in size from small (about 6 or 7 inches) to larger (10 inches). Many come with nonstick coatings.
- **Quiche Pan:** As an alternative to standard pie plates, quiche pans have straight or fluted sides for extra appeal.
- **Ramekins:** These small dishes are perfect for custards, individual casseroles, baked eggs, and other recipes. They are available in an assortment of sizes, from a few ounces all the way to a dozen.
- **Skillets:** Keep an assortment of skillets of different sizes on hand to make a variety of egg dishes. For the most flexibility, be sure some are shallow and others are deep. It's also a good idea to have a nonstick and cast-iron skillet on hand.
- **Soufflé Dish:** This specialty baking dish is a deep casserole dish with high, straight sides and is available in different sizes.
- **Spatula:** Rubber spatulas tend to be the best suited for gently folding egg whites, while metal spatulas are best for flipping fried eggs. Consider purchasing at least one of each to make sure your recipes turn out perfectly. A heat-proof rubber spatula is helpful in scrambling eggs.
- **Whisks:** An assortment of whisks is essential for whipping egg yolks and egg whites by hand. Look for small, medium, and large balloon whisks to ensure you always have the right tool for the recipe.

EGG DISHES FROM AROUND THE WORLD

- **Crème Caramel** (France): This creamy, baked custard dessert is very similar to crème brûlée, except the smooth custard has a soft caramel top instead of a crunchy caramel topping. After baking and cooling, the crème caramel is turned out onto a plate or serving platter and the excess caramel sauce pools around the custard. The most complicated part of this dish is making the caramel. To avoid crystallization, don't stir the sugar and water mixture until all the sugar is dissolved and the caramel is already a light golden color.

- **Eggs Benedict** (USA): A perfect eggs benedict consists of a lightly toasted English muffin topped with Canadian bacon and perfectly poached eggs drenched in a luscious and buttery hollandaise sauce. Hollandaise is made by whisking together warmed, clarified butter with egg yolks.

- **Egg Tart** (China): This small classic dessert is a simple egg custard baked in a cookie or puff pastry crust. Chinese egg tarts are thought to have derived from British custard tarts, but the Chinese version is made without milk and is served piping hot rather than chilled. When baking these tarts, crack the oven slightly at the end of the cooking time to prevent the custard filling from puffing up.

- **Frittata** (Italy): This open-faced omelet is often finished in the oven. It can be filled or topped with meats, cheeses, vegetables, and any leftovers you may have in the refrigerator. Frittatas don't need very much time in the oven or on the stovetop so make sure you warm your topping ingredients or let them come to room temperature so they don't cool the finished dish.

- **Huevos Rancheros** (Mexico): This humble meal combines fried eggs, tortillas, and spicy salsa and comes in many delicious variations. Some versions include cheese, rice, jalapeño peppers, refried beans, salsa verde, and avocado. They can also have poached or scrambled eggs instead of fried. If you choose to use fresh jalapeño peppers, be sure to wear gloves or wash your hands thoroughly after chopping them to prevent the juice from irritating your eyes.

- **Kao Tom** (Thailand): This Thai breakfast dish is very quick to make. It consists of hot chicken or pork and rice soup with ginger and chiles spooned over poached eggs. More complex Kao Toms include shredded vegetables, spices, and other meats. The traditional method to prepare this soup is to crack an egg into a soup bowl and spoon the boiling hot soup over the egg and let the mixture stand about 4 minutes to allow the egg to poach in the hot liquid. The eggs can be poached ahead as well.

- **Meringues** (Switzerland or France): Thought to be a Swiss innovation, meringues are actually more associated with France. A meringue is a combination of stiffly beaten egg whites, sugar, and sometimes cream of tartar. They can be baked into crisp cookies or cake layers, spooned onto pies, and used as a base for other recipes like angel food cake. An Italian-style meringue is made with a boiled sugar syrup that is beaten into the egg whites for a softer finished product. Older egg whites tend to make the best meringues because they whip into a greater volume than fresh eggs.

- **Quiche** (France): This savory egg custard is baked in a pie crust and can be filled with an assortment of ingredients, including bacon, cheese, vegetables, herbs, smoked salmon, and potatoes. Quiche is usually served at room temperature or chilled to allow the custard to set. For the crispiest crust, pre-bake the pie crust before filling it.

- **Scotch Eggs** (England): This recipe has been around for more than two hundred years and is very popular as snacks or pub food. Don't let the idea of these delicious deep-fried eggs sound too daunting to make. They are actually not as difficult to prepare as you might think. To make these, wrap hard-boiled eggs in ground sausage and dredge them in bread crumbs before deep-frying. If the sausage meat is having trouble sticking, roll the eggs in flour first.
- **Tortilla Patatas** (Spain): The name of this Spanish specialty basically translates to "potato pancake." While the classic version contains only eggs, potato, and some seasonings, other ingredients can be added to this dish. They can be served for any meal, including as a tapas dish or snack. When creating *tortilla patatas,* use less starchy potatoes that fry better (such as Yukon Gold) and slice them as thinly as possible.

. . . .

For some of the recipes in this book, you will need to separate the egg whites from the egg yolks. This can be done easily by transferring the egg yolk back and forth between the egg shell halves. You can also use an egg funnel instead. Gently crack the egg into the funnel end. The egg yolks should stay in the top while the whites pass through the funnel.

. . . .

BEYOND WHAT CAME FIRST: FAQ ABOUT EGGS

What is salmonella and how can I avoid it?

Salmonella is a bacteria that can infect chickens and be passed to their eggs as well. Though not necessarily harmful in small amounts, this bacteria can easily grow to dangerous levels if the eggs are not stored, cooked, or cooled correctly. Most cases of salmonella contamination in humans, however, are caused by drinking water or eating food contaminated by animal feces. Salmonella can cause typhoid fever, food poisoning, gastroenteritis, and other diseases. Bacteria is present on the outside shell and can be found less frequently on the inside of eggs. The statistics concerning eggs infected with salmonella are actually quite comforting because only one in about 20,000 eggs might be contaminated, which is about 0.005 percent. If you are an average egg user, you might end up with a salmonella-contaminated egg once in eighty-four years. That being said, there are some precautions you can take to cut your risks even further, including:

- Do not buy eggs that are cracked or visibly dirty.
- Buy eggs that are stored in refrigerated cases.
- If you purchase eggs from a farmer, ensure the farm is clean and well maintained.

- Make sure your own kitchen is clean, and that you thoroughly scrub all areas that come in contact with raw eggs, including your hands.
- Cook your eggs until the whites or yolks are firm and bake casseroles to at least 160°F. If you like runny yolks but are concerned about salmonella, purchase pasteurized eggs. Pasteurized eggs taste a bit different from regular eggs but are a great option for the very young or old and those with compromised immune systems.

Why do hard-boiled eggs sometimes have gray rings around the yolks?

This is a natural reaction when an egg is overcooked because of the iron and sulfur present in the eggs. They are still safe to eat, even with the unattractive appearance. To avoid grey rings, try to cook the eggs for the proper amount of time and chill them quickly after draining to stop the cooking process.

Is there a way to tell if eggs are fresh?

Yes—just break them open. If the yolk is firm and the whites are a bit cloudy and thick, then your eggs are fresh. Or drop the egg carefully into a glass of water. If the egg floats, it probably isn't fresh. Older eggs tend to have more air in the shell.

Can eggs still be eaten after the "best before" date?

The "best before" date is the timeframe that the eggs will still be considered Grade AA quality. When eggs are at their freshest, the whites don't spread out very far and the yolks are high and round. It is not an expiration date. If your eggs have been refrigerated, you can still eat them a short time after the indicated date. Make sure you cook them thoroughly in casseroles or hard-boil them.

Can I use an egg even if the shell is cracked?

If you happen to find that one of your eggs is cracked, you can still use it as long as the egg contents have not leaked out of the shell. If they have leaked, then discard the egg. If the shell is just cracked, then use the egg as soon as possible in a recipe where the egg is fully cooked.

What is the best way to crack an egg?

If you have ever watched cooking shows, you might have seen professional chefs deftly cracking cartons of eggs using one hand. This is a great way to crack eggs, but it takes practice. If you are at the stage where you use two hands to crack your eggs the following technique is a good place to start:

- You should always hold the egg in your dominant hand between your first two fingers and your thumb. When you're breaking an egg, the key is to rap it on the widest part of the shell, around the middle.
- Rap the widest part of the egg firmly against a hard surface—either the edge of a bowl or the countertop.
- Use the thumb of the other hand to gently pry the egg open. Pull the egg halves apart with both hands into a bowl or measuring cup.

- If there are any pieces of shell in your cracked egg, you can easily fish them out by using one of the shell halves or by wetting your fingers.
- To separate the egg yolk from the white, gently transfer the egg yolk between the two egg shell halves, allowing the whites to fall into the bowl. Or, scoop the egg yolk out carefully with your hand and transfer it to another bowl leaving the whites behind.

Are eggs with red spots inside safe to eat?

These eggs are usually weeded out during the inspection process, but they are safe to eat. Red spots are blood from a ruptured blood vessel in the hen when the egg is forming. If the red spot is bothersome, then remove it with the tip of a knife before cooking the egg.

How can you tell if an egg is hard-boiled or raw if you put them back in the refrigerator?

If you are unsure if your egg has been cooked or not, spin it on its side on a flat surface. If it wobbles and spins slowly, it is raw. If it spins quickly and smoothly, it is hard-boiled. You can keep hard-boiled eggs in the refrigerator for up to 1 week in a sealed container.

Should I limit the amount of eggs I eat or only eat egg whites?

There is a school of thought that states egg whites are the healthier part of the egg, but current research has shown that the yolks actually contain even more vitamins and health benefits. While egg whites contain most of the egg's riboflavin and protein without any cholesterol, the yolk also has protein and riboflavin in addition to vitamins D, A, B_6, and B_{12}, and phosphorous, iron, zinc, thiamine, and folic acid. Egg yolks also contain cholesterol and fat, which has given them a bad reputation, but pasture-raised and some free-range eggs contain higher levels of heart-healthy omega-3 fatty acids. Therefore, eating both the whites and the yolks is a great way to get all the nutrients eggs offer, and provided you do not have an issues with high cholesterol, there is no limit to the amount of eggs you can eat. You should still stick to a well-balanced diet, which, according to USDA and Harvard Medical School, might mean limiting your egg consumption to between one and three egg yolks per day, depending on your age and gender.

Studies have shown that eating one egg per day does not increase the likelihood of developing heart disease or stroke in healthy people. One egg contains about half the recommended cholesterol for healthy people, but if you already have an existing condition like heart disease, diabetes, or high cholesterol, consider reducing your egg yolk consumption to be safe. In those cases, egg whites might be the best choice if your doctor recommends limiting cholesterol intake.

CHAPTER THREE

Eggs Quick and Easy

It's easy to save both time and money when cooking delicious egg dishes. Eggs are considered some of the most cost-effective, easy ingredients to work with in the kitchen.

When cooking any recipe, the most important strategy for saving time and money is to plan everything. Think about all the times you might have purchased fast food or pre-made meals because you had no idea what to cook, or all of the produce, meats, and eggs you threw out because they weren't used fast enough. The key to smart, effective cooking (with or without eggs) is to know what you have in your kitchen, make a meal plan using some of those on-hand ingredients, and buy only what is on your list. Obviously, if you use certain nonperishable ingredients regularly and they are on sale, go for the purchase, but resist the impulse to overbuy whenever possible.

. . . .

Planning ahead, prepping ahead, and reducing your waste are the keys to efficient cooking. Try out these tips for shopping, planning meals, preparing, and storing your delicious egg-based meals, and you might just find the time spent in your kitchen to be even more enjoyable and productive.

. . . .

QUICK AND EASY PREPARATION TIPS

1. Always choose the size of egg and quantity that suits your lifestyle and recipe needs. If you live alone and do not use eggs often, buy a half-dozen rather than a full dozen at a time. Purchase large eggs instead of extra-large eggs to further cut back on waste.
2. If eggs are a regular part of your diet, purchase your eggs in larger quantities and hard-boil half of them to have on hand for recipes or snacks. Keep in mind that hard-boiled eggs have a shorter shelf life and last up to 1 week in the refrigerator.
3. Preparation makes everything easier in the kitchen. Prepare all the components of your recipe before you start cooking. Your *mise en place* can also be stored in the refrigerator in sealed containers until ready for use.
4. Never go shopping without planning your meals for the week and try to use leftovers for the next day's breakfast, lunch, or dinner.

5. If you are going to make hard-boiled eggs, consider purchasing the eggs 1 week prior to make peeling easier. Fresh eggs are difficult to peel.

6. Be on the lookout for sales and specials at your grocery store to organize your meals around inexpensive ingredients. Seasonal vegetables are also more inexpensive, so pay attention to what is available. Buy commonly used items like canned diced tomatoes in bulk, especially if you plan to create many meals.

7. When you get home from the store, take a look at your weekly menu and give yourself a head start by washing and chopping the vegetables for your dishes. Store these prepared vegetables in airtight containers in the refrigerator. Only prepare vegetables that hold well and avoid pre-cutting ingredients such as tomatoes, which can become mealy if stored in the fridge ahead of time. Similarly, avocadoes, apples, and other fruit can brown if you prepare them too early.

8. Use your leftovers in other recipes to save money and time. Cooked vegetables, pasta, and meats can easily be used in omelets, frittatas, and egg casseroles.

9. Always clean as you go so you have a clean workspace when cooking and reduced cleanup time. You should also keep your pantry and fridge tidy so you know exactly what is available for your recipes and to help with meal planning.

10. Freeze leftover frittata slices in zip-top plastic bags for a quick meal or snack. You can also cut leftover frittatas into squares or rectangles so they can be used between bread for a sandwich or in a tortilla wrap. Simply pop the square in the microwave for a minute or defrost the frittata portion in the refrigerator overnight.

. . . .

Eggs go through distinct changes as they get older in your fridge, but these changes will not affect their nutritional profile. Older eggs have thinner egg whites with flatter egg yolks more prone to breaking. Fresh eggs are best for poached or fried eggs because the egg holds its shape and the egg yolk sits higher when plated.

. . . .

QUICK AND EASY COOKING TIPS AND TECHNIQUES

1. Prepare the omelet fillings or frittata toppings ahead of time and store them in the refrigerator until you need them. Simply rewarm the ingredients in a small skillet or in the microwave before adding them to the egg dish.

2. Cut filling ingredients into small pieces so that they cook quickly. Or invest in a mandoline to slice and grate vegetables in minutes. Mandoline blades tend to be very sharp, so always use the safety guard when cutting.

3. To save cooking and cleanup time, poach the eggs in sauce instead of water or bake eggs directly in a casserole, rice, or vegetable dish. Make sure your base is very hot to speed up the cooking time.

4. Many egg dishes, like casseroles, can be made in a slow cooker in advance for hands-off cooking. You can also prepare casseroles and baked egg dishes ahead of time and store them, uncooked, in the refrigerator overnight until you are ready to cook them.

5. If you end up with pesky eggshells in your cracked eggs, rather than fishing them out with a fork, simply wet your fingers and pick them out.

6. If a recipe calls for chopped bacon, place the entire piece or package of bacon in the freezer for about 15 minutes to make cutting easier.

7. To make a big batch of hard-boiled eggs, place them directly on the middle rack in your oven and put a rimmed baking sheet on the bottom rack to catch any broken ones. Heat the oven to 325°F and bake the eggs for 30 minutes without preheating the oven. Remove the eggs with tongs or a spoon and transfer them to a bowl of ice water to stop the cooking process.

8. Cook bacon and sausage ahead of time for any egg recipes by placing them on baking trays and baking at 350°F for about 30 minutes, turning occasionally. Store the bacon or sausage in the refrigerator in sealed bags until you are ready to use them.

9. To peel multiple hard-boiled eggs at once, place them in a sealed plastic container and shake for 1 minute or longer. The shells will break up and slip off when you rinse the eggs.

10. When making omelets, be careful not to overstuff them or tear them when folding the omelet in half.

- -

Sometimes it is difficult crack your eggs without getting shells into the mix. This can be very inconvenient if you are breaking eggs into a hot skillet. Instead of breaking the eggs directly into the pan, crack the eggs into a small bowl first so you can get the offending shells out before tipping the eggs into the skillet.

- -

QUICK AND EASY STORAGE TIPS

1. Always store eggs in the coldest part of the refrigerator to prevent bacteria growth and only allow refrigerated eggs to sit out at room temperature for two hours or less.

2. Keep your eggs in the container they are purchased in so you can refer to the "best before" date stamped on the packaging. Also, keep them away from foods that have a strong odor like onions or raw garlic because the shells of eggs are porous and can absorb the scent.

3. Do not store your eggs in the door of the refrigerator because frequent opening will cause fluctuating temperatures and affect safe egg storage.

4. To freeze whole eggs or whites, beat and pour them into an airtight container. Be sure to label and date the container. If you are freezing yolks separately, beat in about 1 teaspoon sugar or

⅛ teaspoon salt for every four yolks because once frozen, egg yolks will thicken. The addition of sugar or salt helps the yolks maintain their structure after they are thawed. Be sure to label, date, and include the contents added to the yolks on the outside of the sealed container or bag.

5. Store leftover frittatas, casseroles, and other cooked egg dishes in the refrigerator completely covered and consume them within two or three days. Discard any egg leftovers after that time.

Don't ignore calls for room temperature eggs in recipes. Cold eggs react differently with other ingredients, especially when baking cakes. Cold eggs don't incorporate well with butter or shortening in batters, which can create a lumpy mess. They also don't reach as much volume as room temperature eggs, which can be crucial for texture in cakes, soufflés, and meringues.

PART TWO

Quick and Easy Egg Recipes

CHAPTER FOUR

Basic Eggs

Learning the basic preparations for cooking eggs will give you a wonderful foundation for preparing many recipes. Eggs are forgiving ingredients in most cases, but when you master various cooking techniques you will be delighted with the array of new textures, tastes, and presentations for this humble food. There are many ways to make eggs but here are the ten most common preparations that can be used alone or as a component in preparing other great dishes.

PERFECT SCRAMBLED EGGS

POACHED EGGS

BASIC OMELET

BAKED EGGS

SOFT-BOILED EGGS

HARD-BOILED EGGS

SUNNY-SIDE UP FRIED EGGS

OVER-EASY FRIED EGGS

OVER-MEDIUM FRIED EGGS

OVER-HARD FRIED EGGS

Perfect Scrambled Eggs

MAKES 2 SERVINGS

Prep time: 5 minutes
Cook time: 5 minutes

Fluffy scrambled eggs are a wonderful treat and can be made with an assortment of additional ingredients such as onions, cheeses, meats, and fresh herbs. Scrambled eggs can overcook easily, so it is important to cook them over lower heat and always supervise the process.

4 EGGS
3 TABLESPOONS WHOLE MILK
1 TABLESPOON BUTTER OR CLARIFIED BUTTER
SEA SALT AND FRESHLY GROUND PEPPER

1. In a small stainless steel or glass bowl, crack the eggs and beat the eggs until they are pale yellow.

2. Add the milk and whisk the mixture vigorously until the eggs are foamy, about 3 minutes.

3. In a medium nonstick skillet over medium-low heat, heat the butter until melted and bubbly.

4. Add the egg mixture and cook until they just start to set, about 30 seconds.

5. With a rubber spatula, gently scrape the set eggs from the edges of the skillet to the center of the skillet to create fluffy curds and to allow the uncooked egg to flow underneath.

6. Continue cooking until there is no liquid left.

7. Remove the skillet from the heat and gently stir the scrambled eggs until they are firm but not dry, being careful not to break them up. Season with salt and pepper.

Poached Eggs

MAKES 2

Prep time: 1 minute
Cook time: 3 to 6 minutes

The eggs may look very strange when you crack them into the simmering water, but as they cook they develop into a wonderful texture. Poached eggs are lovely on sandwiches, salads, with vegetables, and, of course, balanced on toast or English muffins. When poaching, be sure not to overcrowd the saucepan with eggs. Too many eggs poaching at the same time will reduce the temperature of the water and make it difficult to keep the eggs separate.

1 TEASPOON WHITE VINEGAR
2 EGGS

1. Fill a large saucepan with about 4 to 5 inches of water and the vinegar and bring to a boil over high heat.

2. Reduce the heat to medium and maintain a simmer.

3. Crack 1 egg into a small bowl.

4. Gently slip the egg into the simmering water. Repeat the process with the remaining egg.

5. Cook the eggs for about 3 minutes, until the egg whites are firm.

6. Remove the eggs with a slotted spoon and drain on paper towels.

Basic Omelet

Prep time: 2 minutes
Cook time: 5 minutes

It can be tricky to achieve a perfect, fluffy, and pale omelet, but even slightly overcooked omelets are still delicious. This recipe is for a plain omelet, but you can fill it with an assortment of delicious ingredients such as cheese, meats, and vegetables. The fillings should be cooked ahead of time if raw and added right before you fold the omelet in half to create a half-moon shape.

2 EGGS
2 TABLESPOONS WATER OR WHOLE MILK
PINCH OF SEA SALT
DASH OF FRESHLY GROUND PEPPER
1 TEASPOON BUTTER, CLARIFIED BUTTER, OR OIL

1. In a small bowl, whisk together the eggs, water or milk, salt, and pepper until thoroughly combined. Set aside.

2. In a medium nonstick skillet or omelet pan over medium-high heat, heat butter or oil until melted, about 20 seconds, swirling to coat the pan.

3. Pour the egg mixture into the pan and stir gently with a heat-proof spatula or wooden spoon as it starts to set.

4. As the egg begins to set, lift the edges and push them slightly towards the center, allowing the uncooked egg to flow underneath.

5. Continue the process until the eggs are completely cooked and fluffy or almost fully cooked for a creamier center.

6. Flip one side of the omelet over the other to create a half moon and slide the omelet onto a serving plate.

Baked Eggs

MAKES 2

Prep time: 1 minute
Cook time: 10 minutes

These eggs, often called shirred eggs, are usually cooked in individual cups, ramekins, or mugs. You can make many variations of this dish with spinach, salsa, cheese, meats, and even smoked salmon, depending on the occasion and your own preference.

BUTTER OR COOKING SPRAY
2 EGGS
1 TABLESPOON MILK OR WHIPPING CREAM
SEA SALT AND FRESHLY GROUND PEPPER

1. Preheat the oven to 325°F.

2. Use the butter to grease a 10-ounce ramekin.

3. Break the eggs carefully into the ramekin to keep the yolks intact.

4. Spoon the milk or whipping cream over the eggs and season with salt and pepper.

5. Bake the eggs until the egg whites are set and the egg yolks are slightly thickened but still runny, about 10 minutes.

6. Serve immediately.

Soft-Boiled Eggs

MAKES 2

Prep time: 1 minute
Cook time: 6 minutes

There is something luxurious about dipping toast strips or blanched asparagus into a perfectly soft-boiled egg, where the whites are firm and the yolks runny and rich. Timing on these eggs has to be almost perfect so don't get discouraged if it takes a bit of practice to master this technique.

WATER
2 EGGS

1. Fill a large saucepan with about 5 inches of water and bring to a boil over medium-high heat.

2. Reduce the heat to medium and maintain a simmer. With a slotted spoon, lower each egg into the water, 1 at a time.

3. Cook the eggs for exactly 5 minutes and remove them from the water using the slotted spoon.

4. Run the eggs under cold water for about 1 minute.

5. Using a knife, carefully cut off the tip of the egg and eat it straight from the shell.

Hard-Boiled Eggs

Prep time: 1 minute
Cook time: 10 minutes

Hard-boiled eggs are very versatile and can be eaten plain with a sprinkling of pepper and salt or used in many other dishes such as salads and sandwiches.

2 EGGS
WATER

1. In a large saucepan, carefully place the eggs in a single layer. Add enough water to cover the eggs by about 1 inch.

2. Cover and bring the water to a boil over medium-high heat. Remove the saucepan from the heat and let stand, covered, for 10 to 12 minutes.

3. Remove the eggs from the pan with a slotted spoon and run under cold water to cool.

4. Store the cooked, unshelled eggs in the refrigerator for up to 1 week.

Sunny-Side Up Fried Eggs

MAKES 2

Prep time: 1 minute
Cook time: 3 minutes

These eggs are wonderful for breakfast but can also be used to top casseroles, rice dishes, and even burgers, sandwiches, and salads. Fried eggs have a silkier texture and taste when slightly undercooked.

- -

Chef's Tip: Never try to speed up the cooking time on fried eggs to get them cooked faster. Higher heat changes the protein structure of the egg and makes them rubbery with hard brown edges. If you find your egg whites are too runny even after the yolks are to the desired doneness, try covering the skillet for about 30 seconds to steam the eggs without over-browning them.

- -

1 TABLESPOON BUTTER, OIL, OR BACON GREASE
2 EGGS
SEA SALT AND FRESHLY GROUND PEPPER

1. In a small nonstick skillet over medium-high heat, heat the butter, oil, or bacon grease until melted and bubbly.

2. Carefully crack the eggs into the pan, keeping the yolks intact.

3. Cook the eggs, without turning, until the egg whites are completely set and the egg yolks are still runny. Carefully slide the eggs onto a plate and season with salt and pepper.

Over-Easy Fried Eggs

MAKES 2

Prep time: 1 minute
Cook time: 3 minutes

Over-easy eggs are basically fried eggs that are cooked on both sides to briefly cook the outside layer of the yolk while leaving the inside of the yolk runny. Use a flat, wide spatula to flip the eggs easily without breaking the yolk.

1 TABLESPOON BUTTER OR OIL
2 LARGE EGGS
SEA SALT AND FRESHLY GROUND BLACK PEPPER

1. In a small nonstick skillet over medium-high heat, heat the butter or oil until melted and bubbly.

2. Carefully crack the eggs into the pan, keeping the yolks intact.

3. Cook the eggs, without turning, until the egg whites are just set but still runny around the yolk, about 1 to 2 minutes.

4. With a flat, wide spatula, gently turn the eggs over, keeping the egg yolks intact.

5. Continue to cook, for about 2 minutes.

6. Turn the eggs over and slide them onto a serving plate.

7. Season with salt and pepper.

Over-Medium Fried Eggs

MAKES 2

Prep time: 1 minute
Cook time: 3 minutes

Over-medium fried eggs can be tricky to make because the timing has to be precise. The egg yolk should to be soft and still runny when pierced and the egg whites completely cooked.

1 TABLESPOON BUTTER OR OIL
2 EGGS
SEA SALT AND FRESHLY GROUND PEPPER

1. In a small nonstick skillet over medium-high heat, heat the butter or oil until melted and bubbly.

2. Carefully crack the eggs into the skillet, keeping the yolks intact.

3. Cook the eggs, without turning, until the egg whites are just set but still runny around the yolk, about 1 to 2 minutes.

4. With a flat, wide spatula, gently turn the eggs over, keeping the egg yolks intact.

5. Continue to cook, about 1 minute.

6. Turn the eggs over and slide them onto a plate.

7. Season with salt and pepper.

Over-Hard Fried Eggs

MAKES 2

Prep time: 1 minute
Cook time: 5 minutes

Over-hard fried eggs are perfect for those who don't enjoy runny yolks. The trick with these is to cook the eggs slowly so that the texture is still soft but not rubbery.

1 TABLESPOON BUTTER OR OIL
2 EGGS
SEA SALT AND FRESHLY GROUND PEPPER

1. In a small nonstick skillet over medium-high heat, heat the butter or oil until melted and bubbly.

2. Carefully crack the eggs into the pan, keeping the egg yolks intact.

3. Reduce the heat to low.

4. Cook the eggs, without turning, until the egg whites are opaque and the yolk is completely firm, about 5 minutes.

5. Season with salt and pepper.

6. Serve immediately.

CHAPTER FIVE

Sauces and Dressings

Hollandaise

Prep time: 20 minutes
Cook time: 20 minutes

This is one of the silkiest, most luscious sauces around. Though hollandaise is actually quite simple to make, you must have a little patience and a good wire whisk. Make the clarified butter portion ahead to save a bit of time. Simply follow the recipe instructions and store your clarified butter in a sealed container in the refrigerator for up to 3 weeks.

1½ CUPS UNSALTED BUTTER
4 EGG YOLKS
2 TEASPOONS COLD WATER
4 TEASPOONS FRESHLY SQUEEZED LEMON JUICE (ABOUT 1 LEMON)
PINCH OF SEA SALT

1. In a medium heavy-bottomed saucepan over low heat, melt the butter.

2. Remove the saucepan from the heat, and let stand for 5 minutes.

3. Carefully skim off the top layer of foam and discard.

4. Slowly pour the clear yellow clarified butter into a container, leaving the milky solids in the bottom of the saucepan. Discard the milky solids, and let the clarified butter stand at room temperature until it is just warm, about 20 minutes.

5. Fill a medium saucepan with about 3 inches of water and bring to a simmer over medium heat.

6. In a large stainless steel bowl, whisk together the egg yolks and 2 teaspoons cold water until foamy and light, about 3 minutes.

7. Add 3 to 4 drops of the lemon juice and whisk for about 1 minute.

8. Place the bowl over the saucepan of simmering water, making sure the bottom of the bowl does not touch the water.

9. Whisk the egg yolk mixture until slightly thickened, about 1 to 2 minutes. Remove the bowl from the heat, and set aside.

10. Slowly add the clarified butter to the egg yolk mixture in a very thin stream, whisking constantly, until the sauce is thick and smooth. (Adding the butter too quickly can cause the sauce to break.) Whisk in the remaining lemon juice and season with salt.

11. Serve immediately.

Béarnaise Sauce

MAKES 2 CUPS

Prep time: 10 minutes
Cook time: 30 minutes

If you are looking for the perfect egg-based sauce for vegetables, fish, or filet mignon, this is a delicious, elegant choice. Béarnaise is flavored with tarragon, which might not be an herb you have in your kitchen, but it is worth trying in this and other dishes. Use dried tarragon in the recipe if you cannot find fresh. The flavor of dried tarragon is less intense because the essential oils in the herb dissipate when dried.

Chef's Tip: *If you have difficulty finding fresh tarragon where you live, buy extra when you do see it because tarragon freezes well. Simply place whole sprigs in plastic zip-top freezer bags and freeze for up to 5 months; there is no need to thaw it.*

1½ CUPS UNSALTED BUTTER
½ CUP WHITE WINE VINEGAR
4 TEASPOONS FINELY CHOPPED SHALLOTS
½ TEASPOON CRUSHED PEPPERCORNS
2 TEASPOONS CHOPPED FRESH TARRAGON
4 EGG YOLKS
2 TEASPOONS CHOPPED FRESH PARSLEY
JUICE OF ½ LEMON
PINCH OF CAYENNE PEPPER
PINCH OF SEA SALT

1. In a medium, heavy-bottomed saucepan over low heat, melt the butter.

2. Remove the saucepan from the heat, and let stand for 5 minutes.

3. Carefully skim off the top layer of foam and discard.

4. Slowly pour the clear yellow, clarified butter into a container leaving the milky solids in the bottom of the saucepan. Discard the milky solids, and let the clarified butter stand at room temperature until it is just warm, about 20 minutes.

5. In a small saucepan over medium-high heat, bring the vinegar, shallots, peppercorns, and 1 teaspoon of the tarragon to a simmer. Simmer for 3 to 5 minutes or until the mixture is reduced to about 2 tablespoons liquid.

6. Transfer the vinegar mixture to a medium stainless steel bowl. Add the egg yolks, and whisk until foamy and light, about 3 minutes.

7. Fill a medium saucepan with about 3 inches of water and bring to a simmer over medium heat.

8. Place the bowl over the saucepan of simmering water, making sure the bottom of the bowl does not touch the water.

9. Whisk the egg yolk mixture until slightly thickened, about 1 to 2 minutes. Remove the bowl from the heat and set aside.

10. Slowly add the clarified butter to the egg yolk mixture in a very thin stream, whisking constantly, until the sauce is thick and smooth. (Adding the butter too quickly can cause the sauce to break.)

11. Transfer the sauce to a new bowl and stir in the remaining tarragon.Whisk in the parsley, lemon juice, and cayenne pepper. Season with salt.

12. Serve immediately.

Mayonnaise

MAKES 2 CUPS

Prep time: 5 minutes

If you have never compared the taste and texture of homemade mayonnaise to store-bought, this recipe will be a real eye opener. This recipe calls for raw egg yolks, so if you are concerned about salmonella, use pasteurized eggs or fresh eggs bought the same day or the day before. If you want to substitute a liquid egg product that has been pasteurized, use ½ cup in this recipe as a substitute for 2 whole eggs. If you don't have a food processor, it's easy to make this recipe by hand.

Chef's Tip: *If your mayonnaise breaks or curdles, you can easily fix it by adding another egg yolk or hot water. Beat the additional yolk and slowly pour it into the curdled mayonnaise, whisking constantly, until the mixture is thick and smooth. You can also drip very hot water (about 1 tablespoon) into the curdled mayonnaise, whisking until smooth.*

2 EGGS

2 TABLESPOONS DIJON MUSTARD

1½ CUPS CANOLA OR OLIVE OIL

¼ CUP FRESHLY SQUEEZED LEMON JUICE

SEA SALT AND FRESHLY GROUND PEPPER

To make by hand:

1. In a large bowl, whisk together the eggs and mustard until thoroughly combined.

2. Add the oil in a continuous, thin stream, whisking constantly, until the mixture is thick and completely emulsified.

3. Add the lemon juice and whisk until blended well.

4. Season with salt and pepper.

5. Store the mayonnaise in an airtight container in the refrigerator for up to 4 days.

To make using a food processor:

1. In the bowl of a food processor, add the eggs and mustard. Process until smooth.

2. With the processor running, slowly add the oil in a continuous, thin stream until the mixture is thick and completely emulsified.

3. Add the lemon juice and process until smooth.

4. Season with salt and pepper.

5. Store the mayonnaise in an airtight container in the refrigerator for up to 4 days.

Aioli

MAKES 2½ CUPS

Prep time: 10 minutes

This version of mayonnaise tastes great on roasted meats, fish, and as a sandwich condiment. The classic Provençal condiment got its name from the French word for garlic, ail, *and oil,* oli. *For an even lovelier version, try roasting the garlic first.*

. . . .

Chef's Tip: *This recipe uses a blend of two different oils so that the assertive taste of olive oil does not overpower the flavor of the mayonnaise. Be sure to use regular olive oil in this recipe instead of extra-virgin to help prevent the possibility of breaking.*

. . . .

3 GARLIC CLOVES, PEELED
1 TABLESPOON DIJON MUSTARD
2 EGGS
1 CUP OLIVE OIL
1 CUP CANOLA OIL
2 TABLESPOONS FRESHLY SQUEEZED LEMON JUICE
SEA SALT

To make by hand:

1. Finely mince the garlic.

2. In a large bowl, whisk together the garlic, mustard, and eggs until thoroughly combined.

3. Add the olive oil in a continuous, thin stream, whisking constantly, until the mixture is slightly thickened.

4. Add the canola oil in a continuous, thin stream, whisking constantly, until the mixture is thick and completely emulsified.

5. Add the lemon juice and whisk until blended well.

6. Season with salt.

7. Store the aioli in an airtight container in the refrigerator for up to 4 days.

To make using a food processor:

1. In the bowl of a food processor, combine the garlic, mustard, and eggs. Process until smooth.

2. With the processor running, slowly add the olive oil in a continuous, thin stream until the mixture is slightly thickened.

3. Add the canola oil in a thin, continuous stream until the mixture is thick and completely emulsified.

4. Add the lemon juice and process until smooth.

5. Season with salt.

6. Store the aioli in an airtight container in the refrigerator for up to 4 days.

Creamy Caesar Dressing

MAKES 1½ CUPS

Prep time: 10 minutes
Cook time: 5 minutes

This recipe is a cooked version of the classic garlicky dressing that used to be made tableside in fine-dining restaurants all over the world. This simple variation is delicious, but for an authentic-tasting Caesar dressing, add a ½ cup of freshly grated Parmesan cheese and 1 teaspoon of anchovy paste.

2 GARLIC CLOVES, MINCED
4 EGG YOLKS
¼ CUP WHITE WINE VINEGAR
½ TEASPOON DRY MUSTARD
DASH OF WORCESTERSHIRE SAUCE
1 CUP OLIVE OIL
¼ CUP FRESHLY SQUEEZED LEMON JUICE
SEA SALT AND FRESHLY GROUND PEPPER

1. In a small saucepan over low heat, combine the garlic, egg yolks, vinegar, mustard, and Worcestershire sauce.

2. Cook, whisking constantly, until the egg mixture thickens and bubbles slightly at the edges, about 5 minutes.

3. Remove the saucepan from the heat, and let it stand about 10 minutes to cool.

4. Transfer the egg mixture to a large stainless steel bowl. Slowly add the olive oil in a continuous, thin stream, whisking constantly.

5. Whisk in the lemon juice, and season with salt and pepper.

6. Store the dressing in an airtight container in the refrigerator for up to 3 days.

CHAPTER SIX

Appetizers, Snacks, and Soups

Grilled Egg-Stuffed Mushrooms

MAKES 12 SERVINGS

Prep time: 10 minutes
Cook time: 5 minutes

If you do not have a grill or the weather is not ideal, you can make this dish in your oven using the broiler. Just be sure to broil the mushrooms on both sides before cracking the eggs into them. To save time, you can even cook the mushrooms ahead. Simply store the cooked mushrooms in an airtight container in the refrigerator for up to 2 days. Allow them to come to room temperature before finishing the dish with the eggs.

12 LARGE PORTOBELLO MUSHROOMS, STEMMED
3 TABLESPOONS OLIVE OIL
12 SMALL EGGS
SEA SALT AND FRESHLY GROUND PEPPER
3 TABLESPOONS CHOPPED FRESH CHIVES

1. Preheat the grill to medium-high heat.

2. Use a spoon to remove the gills of the mushroom, carefully scooping to create a ¼-inch-deep cavity.

3. Drizzle the mushrooms with olive oil, then place them hollow-side-up and grill for about 2 minutes.

4. Carefully crack an egg into each of the mushroom cavities.

5. Cover with the grill lid and grill the mushrooms until the egg whites are cooked through, about 2 to 3 minutes.

6. Remove the mushrooms from the grill and season with salt and pepper. Sprinkle with chives just before serving.

Classic Deviled Eggs

MAKES 2 DOZEN

Prep time: 20 minutes

It is a rare picnic or potluck event that does not feature deviled eggs in some variation. This is a basic recipe that can be tweaked for countless different types of deviled eggs. Some ingredients to add to the yolk filling for variety include curry powder, chili powder, pesto, honey mustard, bacon bits, smoked salmon, and chopped black olives. You can also substitute sour cream or yogurt for the mayonnaise, if you'd like.

. . . .

Chef's Tip: *For deviled eggs with a professional look, pipe the filling into the egg white halves with a piping bag fitted with a star tip. Be sure to omit the green onion in the filling to prevent clogs. Instead, use the chopped green onion along with the paprika for garnishing.*

. . . .

12 LARGE HARD-BOILED EGGS (PAGE 35), PEELED
¾ CUP MAYONNAISE (PAGE 46 OR STORE-BOUGHT)
1 TABLESPOON DIJON MUSTARD
¼ CUP CHOPPED GREEN ONION
SEA SALT AND FRESHLY GROUND PEPPER
PAPRIKA FOR GARNISHING

1. Carefully cut the eggs in half lengthwise.

2. Place the egg yolks in a small bowl. Arrange the egg white halves on a serving plate or cutting board.

3. Mash the egg yolks with a fork. Add the mayonnaise, Dijon mustard, and green onion; mix well.

4. Season with salt and pepper.

5. Spoon about 1 tablespoon of the egg yolk mixture into each egg white half.

6. Sprinkle with paprika.

7. Serve immediately, or cover and refrigerate the eggs for about 2 hours to allow the flavors to blend.

Pickled Eggs

MAKES 10 PICKLED EGGS

Prep time: 5 minutes
Cook time: 15 minutes

Many people are not too enchanted with pickled eggs because they used to be a fixture in bars and pubs in large murky jars by the cash register. Fresh homemade pickled eggs are a different thing altogether! Add about ½ cup of beet juice to the pickling liquid in this recipe to create vibrant pink eggs that contrast beautifully with the yellow yolks.

1½ CUPS WHITE VINEGAR
1 CUP SUGAR
1 TABLESPOON WHOLE ALLSPICE
1 CINNAMON STICK, BROKEN IN HALF
10 HARD-BOILED EGGS (PAGE 35), PEELED

1. In a medium saucepan over medium-high heat, combine the vinegar, sugar, allspice, and cinnamon.

2. Bring the mixture to a boil, and stir until the sugar is dissolved, about 5 minutes.

3. Reduce the heat to low and simmer the mixture for 5 minutes.

4. Place the eggs in a large (1-quart) jar, and pour the hot liquid over the eggs.

5. Cover the jar tightly with a lid and let stand for at least 1 hour, or until the liquid reaches room temperature.

6. Store in the refrigertator for up to 3 months.

Bacon and Egg Dip

MAKES 2 CUPS

Prep time: 15 minutes
Cook time: 10 minutes

This dip is both decadent and completely addictive. You might find yourself simply eating it with a spoon. Use this as a tasty sandwich or wrap filling; because it's so rich you will only need a thin layer. To help with prep time, cook the bacon ahead and store it in the refrigerator until ready to use.

Chef's Tip: *Fresh eggs are more difficult to peel than those that have been stored in the refrigerator for up to 1 week. Obtain your eggs ahead of time and store them in the fridge to allow the egg membranes to separate from the shell a little.*

½ CUP MAYONNAISE (PAGE 46 OR STORE-BOUGHT)
¼ CUP PLAIN YOGURT OR SOUR CREAM
8 SLICES BACON, COOKED AND CRUMBLED
8 HARD-BOILED EGGS (PAGE 35), PEELED AND GRATED
1 GREEN ONION, CHOPPED
PINCH OF CAYENNE PEPPER
SEA SALT AND FRESHLY GROUND BLACK PEPPER
PAPRIKA FOR GARNISHING
1 ROUND LOAF DARK RYE BREAD

1. In a medium bowl, combine the mayonnaise, yogurt, bacon, eggs, onion, and cayenne pepper until blended well.

2. Season with salt and pepper.

3. Transfer the dip to a serving bowl and sprinkle with paprika.

4. Cover the dip and store in the refrigerator until ready to serve.

5. Just before serving, cut the bread into cubes and arrange around the dip.

Spicy Cheese and Olive Squares

MAKES 16 SQUARES

Prep time: 10 minutes
Cook time: 20 minutes

If you need a never-fail, always-loved recipe for events and get-togethers, this might be the recipe for you. It is simple to make and has a festive appearance. Customize these tasty squares with some of your favorite ingredients. Green olives, a variety of cheeses, roasted red peppers, sausage, ham, or chicken are great options.

Chef's Tip: *These squares also make a very nice frittata-like filling for wraps or sandwiches. To make these ahead, make and bake as directed, then cover and chill or freeze. To reheat, microwave for about 1 minute or place them in an oven on low heat until they reach the desired temperature.*

OLIVE OIL COOKING SPRAY

1 TEASPOON OLIVE OIL

1 SMALL SWEET ONION, FINELY CHOPPED

1 TEASPOON MINCED GARLIC

4 EGGS

1 CUP GRATED SHARP CHEDDAR CHEESE

½ CUP SLICED BLACK OLIVES

¼ CUP DRY BREAD CRUMBS

3 TABLESPOONS CANNED DICED GREEN CHILES

2 TABLESPOONS FINELY CHOPPED FRESH CILANTRO

PINCH OF SEA SALT

PINCH OF FRESHLY GROUND PEPPER

DASH OF HOT PEPPER SAUCE

1. Preheat the oven to 325°F.

2. Coat an 8-inch square baking dish with cooking spray; set aside.

3. In a medium skillet over medium heat, heat the oil and sauté the onion and garlic for 3 minutes, or until soft.

4. Remove the skillet from the heat.

5. In a medium bowl, whisk together the onion and garlic mixture, eggs, cheese, olives, bread crumbs, chiles, cilantro, salt, pepper, and hot sauce until thoroughly combined.

6. Pour the mixture into the prepared baking pan, and bake for 20 minutes or until a toothpick inserted into the center comes out clean.

7. Let cool for 3 to 5 minutes and cut into 16 squares.

Hot and Sour Soup

MAKES 4 SERVINGS

Prep time: 5 minutes
Cook time: 25 minutes

If you are looking for a meal to perk up your appetite, fight a cold, or aid in digestion, hot and sour soup is a traditional remedy. It is also absolutely delicious when you are perfectly healthy! This soup is even better the next day because the vegetables and tofu have the chance to soak up the complex flavors.

1 TEASPOON ASIAN SESAME OIL

1 CUP SLICED BUTTON OR CREMINI MUSHROOMS

1 TEASPOON GRATED FRESH GINGER

1 CUP CHOPPED COOKED CHICKEN

8 CUPS LOW-SODIUM CHICKEN BROTH

1 TEASPOON SUGAR

4 TEASPOONS RICE VINEGAR

4 TEASPOONS LOW-SODIUM SOY SAUCE

PINCH OF RED PEPPER FLAKES

½ TEASPOON FRESHLY GROUND PEPPER

2 EGGS

4 BABY BOK CHOY, THINLY SLICED

1 CUP FIRM TOFU, CUT INTO ½-INCH CUBES

2 GREEN ONIONS, FINELY CHOPPED

1. In a large stockpot over medium heat, heat the sesame oil and cook the mushrooms and ginger 3 minutes or until the mushrooms are tender.

2. Add the chicken and cook for 1 to 2 minutes, stirring constantly. Add the chicken broth.

3. In a small bowl, whisk together the sugar, rice vinegar, soy sauce, red pepper flakes, and pepper. Stir into the soup mixture.

4. Season the soup with additional vinegar or red pepper flakes, if desired.

5. Bring the soup to a boil over medium-high heat.

6. In a small bowl, whisk the eggs and slowly pour them into the soup in a slow, steady stream, stirring to break up the eggs as they cook in the liquid.

7. Reduce the heat to medium-low, and add the bok choy and tofu.

8. Simmer for about 5 minutes and remove the pot from the heat.

9. Sprinkle each serving with green onion.

Egg Drop Soup

MAKES 4 SERVINGS

Prep time: 5 minutes
Cook time: 10 minutes

This light soup can be on the table in about 15 minutes, making it a great choice when you are in a hurry. Instead of spinach, you can substitute shredded bok choy, bean sprouts, thinly sliced carrots, or any other vegetable, depending on your preference and fridge contents. Be sure the vegetables are cut very finely so that they cook quickly and evenly in the simmering broth.

6 CUPS LOW-SODIUM CHICKEN BROTH
2 CUPS THINLY SLICED SPINACH
¼ TEASPOON GROUND NUTMEG
4 EGGS, BEATEN
¼ CUP GRATED PARMESAN CHEESE
PINCH OF FRESHLY GROUND PEPPER

1. In a large saucepan over medium heat, bring the broth to a simmer.

2. Add the spinach and simmer for 5 minutes, or until wilted. Add the nutmeg.

3. While stirring the soup, add the eggs in a slow, steady stream, breaking them up as they cook. Remove the soup from the heat.

4. Sprinkle each serving with Parmesan cheese and pepper.

CHAPTER SEVEN

Salads

Greens with Egg, Nuts, and Veggies

MAKES 2 LARGE SERVINGS

Prep time: 10 minutes

Cook time: 10 minutes

The ingredients in this salad are packed with protein and healthy omega-3 fatty acids—perfect if you are working out or participating in an active sport. Try this salad for lunch before a big game or for dinner after a long day to allow your body to recuperate and recharge.

Timesaving Tip: *Make the hard-boiled eggs and the dressing ahead of time and store them in separate sealed containers, in the refrigerator, until ready to use.*

3 HARD-BOILED EGGS (PAGE 35)

½ CUP FRESHLY SQUEEZED LEMON JUICE

3 TABLESPOONS OLIVE OIL

3 TEASPOONS GRAINY DIJON MUSTARD

SEA SALT AND FRESHLY GROUND PEPPER

2 CUPS LOOSELY PACKED SPINACH

3 CUPS LOOSELY PACKED ARUGULA

1 CUP GREEN BEANS, TRIMMED AND CUT INTO 1-INCH PIECES

1 CUP HALVED GRAPE TOMATOES

1 SMALL RIPE AVOCADO, PEELED, PITTED, AND DICED

½ CUP PECAN HALVES

1. Peel and quarter the eggs; set aside.

2. In a small bowl, whisk together the lemon juice, olive oil, and mustard. Season with salt and pepper; set aside.

3. Place the spinach and arugula in a medium bowl and add the dressing, tossing to coat.

4. Divide the greens evenly among two plates. Top with the green beans, tomatoes, avocado, and egg quarters.

5. Sprinkle with pecan halves just before serving.

Potato and Egg Salad

MAKES 6 SERVINGS

Prep time: 15 minutes
Cook time: 15 minutes

Potato salad has many different variations, depending on the geographic region and the preference of the cook. This version can be modified easily when the impulse strikes you. Try grated carrot, chopped bacon, jalapeño peppers, pesto, chopped sun-dried tomatoes, and a plethora of different herbs to satisfy your creative streak.

3 POUNDS NEW POTATOES, HALVED
6 HARD-BOILED EGGS (PAGE 35)
¾ CUP MAYONNAISE (PAGE 46 OR STORE-BOUGHT)
1 TABLESPOON DIJON MUSTARD
3 GREEN ONIONS, CHOPPED
4 LARGE DILL PICKLES, FINELY DICED
SEA SALT AND FRESHLY GROUND PEPPER

1. Put the potatoes in a large pot and cover with cold water.

2. Over medium-high heat, bring the water to a boil. Boil the potatoes for 12 to 15 minutes, or until fork-tender.

3. Drain and rinse the potatoes under cold water; set aside to cool.

4. Put the cooled potatoes in a large bowl.

5. Peel and grate the hard-boiled eggs using a box grater; add the egg to the potatoes.

6. Add the mayonnaise, mustard, green onions, and dill pickle; stir to combine thoroughly.

7. Season with salt and pepper.

8. Cover and refrigerate for 2 hours to allow the flavors to blend.

Bacon-Topped Romaine Salad

MAKES 4 APPETIZER SERVINGS OR 2 MAIN COURSE SERVINGS

Prep time: 10 minutes
Cook time: 15 minutes

The dressing in this salad is poured warm over the greens for a delicious, slightly wilted dish perfect for cool weather. Romaine lettuce is robust in texture and complements the dressing well, but spinach or Swiss chard are equally as nice.

Timesaving Tip: *Make the croutons up to one week ahead. Either brown them in olive oil or leftover bacon drippings in a skillet or toast them in the oven. Store the croutons in an airtight container until ready to use.*

6 SLICES THICK CUT BACON

1 LARGE HEAD ROMAINE LETTUCE, TORN INTO BITE-SIZE PIECES

3 HARD-BOILED EGGS (PAGE 35), PEELED AND COARSELY CHOPPED

TWO 1-INCH-THICK SLICES DAY-OLD FRENCH OR ITALIAN CRUSTY BREAD, CUT INTO ½-INCH CUBES

2 TABLESPOONS OLIVE OIL

3 SHALLOTS, MINCED

½ TEASPOON MINCED GARLIC

2 TABLESPOONS BALSAMIC VINEGAR

SEA SALT AND FRESH GROUND PEPPER

1. Place the bacon in a heavy skillet over medium high heat, and cook for 10 minutes, or until crisp, stirring occasionally.

2. Transfer the cooked bacon to paper towels to drain, reserving the bacon drippings in the skillet.

3. Coarsely chop the bacon.

4. In a large bowl, combine the romaine lettuce, egg, and bacon.

5. Add the bread cubes to the skillet over medium heat and sauté until they are browned. Transfer the croutons to a plate and set aside.

6. Add the oil, shallot, and garlic to the skillet and increase the temperature to medium-high heat. Cook 3 minutes, stirring constantly,until the shallot and garlic are soft and translucent.

7. Add the vinegar and cook for about 10 seconds. Remove the skillet from the heat and let stand for 5 minutes.

8. Pour the warm dressing over the romaine, egg, and bacon. Toss to combine and season with salt and pepper.

9. Add the croutons and serve immediately.

Sausage and Soft-Boiled Egg Salad

MAKES 4 SERVINGS

Prep time: 15 minutes
Cook time: 15 minutes

The warm, runny yolks from the egg in this salad make it extra rich and decadent. Serve this hearty side dish with barbecued chicken or steak. For a vegetarian version, omit the sausage and add an additional teaspoon of olive oil to the ingredients. The entire salad can be made the day before and topped with the poached eggs just before serving.

2 POUNDS BABY NEW POTATOES, HALVED

2 CUPS GREEN BEANS, TRIMMED AND HALVED

3 LINKS MILD OR HOT ITALIAN SAUSAGE, COOKED AND SLICED

1 TABLESPOON OLIVE OIL

1 TEASPOON MINCED GARLIC

2 TABLESPOONS SHERRY VINEGAR

1 CUP HALVED CHERRY OR GRAPE TOMATOES

1 TABLESPOON CHOPPED FRESH PARSLEY

SEA SALT AND FRESHLY GROUND PEPPER

4 EGGS

1. Put the potatoes in a large pot and cover with cold water.

2. Over medium-high heat, bring the water to a boil. Boil the potatoes for 12 minutes or until fork-tender. Add the green beans during the last 2 minutes of cooking.

3. Drain and rinse the vegetables under cold running water to cool. Transfer to a large bowl.

4. Heat a large skillet over medium-high heat. Add the sausage slices and cook for 2 minutes or until lightly browned.

5. Remove the sausage from the skillet with a slotted spoon and add to the potatoes and green beans.

6. Add the olive oil and garlic to the skillet and sauté for 1 minute.

7. Remove the skillet from the heat and stir in the vinegar.

8. Add the tomatoes and parsley to the potatoes, green beans, and sausage. Toss to combine.

9. Pour the dressing from the skillet over the salad and toss to combine.

10. Season with salt and pepper. Divide the salad evenly among 4 serving plates.

11. In a small pot over medium heat, bring water to a simmer.

12. Add the eggs and cook for 6 minutes. Remove the eggs from the pot and let stand at room temperature 2 minutes to cool.

13. Peel the eggs carefully and place 1 egg on each salad.

Sunny Quinoa Salad

MAKES 6 SERVINGS

Prep time: 10 minutes
Cook time: 30 minutes

Quinoa is a popular ingredient in many cuisines because it is versatile and very healthy. It was a staple for the Incas for almost 5,000 years and was considered sacred. Protein-packed, low-calorie quinoa is often thought of as a grain because it is cooked like one, but it is actually the seed from a vegetable from the Swiss chard and spinach family.

Chef's Tip: *Be sure to rinse the quinoa to remove the bitter saponin coating before cooking. This natural coating prevents birds from eating the seeds. In some areas of South America, the saponin-laced water from rinsing quinoa is used to wash clothes.*

1 CUP UNCOOKED QUINOA, RINSED
2 CUPS WATER
1 TEASPOON TURMERIC
4 HARD-BOILED EGGS (PAGE 35), PEELED AND CHOPPED
1 LARGE SWEET POTATO, COOKED AND DICED
½ SMALL SWEET ONION, DICED
1 CUP SPINACH, THINLY SLICED
½ CUP ROASTED UNSALTED SUNFLOWER SEEDS
⅓ CUP CRUMBLED LOW-SODIUM FETA CHEESE
1 TABLESPOON BALSAMIC VINEGAR
2 TABLESPOONS CHOPPED FRESH PARSLEY

1. In a medium saucepan, combine the quinoa, water, and turmeric.

2. Over high heat, bring the water to a boil; reduce the heat to low and simmer, covered, for 15 minutes.

3. Remove the pan from the heat and let stand for 5 to 10 minutes.

4. Transfer the quinoa to a large bowl and add the remaining ingredients. Toss to combine.

5. Cover and refrigerate for at least 2 hours to cool the quinoa and allow the flavors to blend.

CHAPTER EIGHT

Boiled, Poached, and Fried

Tomato Poached Eggs

Prep time: 5 minutes
Cook time: 25 minutes

Almost every country, including China and those in the Middle East, has some sort of dish celebrating this tasty pairing of eggs and tomatoes. Poaching the eggs in the savory tomato sauce is a perfect way to enjoy these two ingredients. Even better, this dish is made in one pan, so cleanup is quick and easy! Serve these eggs over English muffins or toast.

. . . .

Timesaving Tip: *The tomato sauce can be made in advance and reheated when you want to make this dish. If you are really strapped for time, substitute your favorite prepared tomato sauce for the home-made version, as long as it is chunky and low in sodium.*

. . . .

1 TEASPOON OLIVE OIL
1 SMALL SWEET ONION, CHOPPED
ONE 28-OUNCE CAN DICED TOMATOES
1 TEASPOON CHOPPED FRESH BASIL
4 EGGS
SEA SALT AND FRESHLY GROUND PEPPER

1. In a large skillet over medium heat, heat the oil. Add the onion and sauté for 3 minutes or until the onion is translucent.

2. Add the tomatoes and basil. Bring the mixture to a boil and crush the tomatoes with the back of a spoon; reduce the heat to low. Simmer for 10 minutes, stirring occasionally, until most of the liquid has evaporated.

3. With the back of a spoon, make 4 deep wells in the tomato mixture and carefully crack 1 egg into each well.

4. Cover and simmer about 5 to 7 minutes or until the egg whites are cooked but the egg yolks are still runny.

5. Remove the skillet from the heat and season with salt and pepper.

Easy Eggs Florentine

Prep time: 10 minutes
Cook time: 15 minutes

This gorgeous dish has deep-green spinach and snowy white and sunny yellow eggs. The wilted spinach creates a perfect nest for the poached eggs. Try kale, Swiss chard, or even beet greens for interesting variations to the spinach. If you make a substitution, increase the cooking time for wilting the greens.

1 TEASPOON OLIVE OIL
1 CUP SLICED BUTTON OR CREMINI MUSHROOMS
1 SMALL SWEET ONION, CHOPPED
2 TEASPOONS MINCED GARLIC
4 TEASPOONS ALL-PURPOSE FLOUR
2 CUPS 2 PERCENT MILK
2 TEASPOONS DIJON MUSTARD
SEA SALT AND FRESHLY GROUND PEPPER
1 CUP PACKED CHOPPED FRESH SPINACH
8 EGGS

1. In a large skillet over medium heat, heat the oil.

2. Add the mushrooms, onion, and garlic and sauté for 4 to 5 minutes or until tender.

3. Stir in the flour and cook another 2 more minutes.

4. Stir in the milk and cook for 3 minutes, or until the sauce thickens and comes to a boil.

5. Add the Dijon mustard and season with salt and pepper.

6. Stir in the spinach. Once the mixture reaches a simmer, reduce the heat to low.

7. Make 8 deep wells in the spinach mixture and crack 1 egg into each well.

8. Cover and simmer for 6 to 8 minutes or until the egg whites are cooked but the egg yolks are still runny.

Classic Egg Salad

MAKES 2 CUPS

Prep time: 10 minutes
Cook time: 15 minutes

To make this egg salad in a hurry, use an express technique and simply crack the eggs into simmering water and cook them about 5 minutes, or until the yolks and whites are cooked through. You can also use a potato masher or pastry blender instead of the box grater to grate the eggs. This recipe can easily be doubled or tripled to serve a large crowd for a special occasion or get-together.

8 HARD-BOILED EGGS (PAGE 35), PEELED
½ CUP MAYONNAISE
1 TABLESPOON DIJON MUSTARD
2 GREEN ONIONS, CHOPPED
PINCH OF GARLIC POWDER
SEA SALT AND FRESHLY GROUND PEPPER

1. With a box grater, grate the eggs into a medium bowl.

2. Add the mayonnaise, mustard, green onion, and garlic powder.

3. Season with salt and pepper.

4. Store in a sealed container in the refrigerator for up to 5 days.

Huevos Rancheros

MAKES 4 SERVINGS

Prep time: 10 minutes
Cook time: 10 minutes

This humble dish translates to "eggs country-style" and is a hearty meal with all its components, like black beans. Black beans support a healthy cardiovascular and digestive system and can help stabilize blood sugar.

FOUR 8-INCH CORN TORTILLAS
1 TABLESPOON OLIVE OIL
8 EGGS
1 CUP FRESH SALSA
1 CUP CANNED BLACK BEANS, DRAINED AND RINSED
1 CUP SOUR CREAM
1 CUP GRATED SHARP CHEDDAR CHEESE
4 TEASPOONS CHOPPED FRESH CILANTRO

1. Preheat the oven to 200°F.

2. Wrap the tortillas in a clean kitchen towel and place them in the oven to warm.

3. In a large skillet over medium-high heat, heat ½ tablespoon of the oil.

4. Crack 4 of the eggs in the skillet and cook for 4 minutes, or until the egg whites are set and the yolks are runny.

5. Transfer the cooked eggs to a baking sheet and place in the oven to keep warm.

6. Repeat the process with the remaining oil and eggs.

7. On a clean work surface, arrange the tortillas in a single layer. Spread 2 tablespoons of the salsa onto each tortilla. Top each with ¼ cup of the black beans.

8. Place 2 eggs on each tortilla. Spoon 1 tablespoon of salsa, 2 tablespoons sour cream, 2 tablespoons cheese, and ½ teaspoon cilantro over each egg.

9. Serve immediately.

Open-Faced Egg Sandwiches

MAKES 4 SERVINGS

Prep time: 5 minutes
Cook time: 5 minutes

These pretty sandwiches would not be out of place on the patio of a charming bistro in Italy. The sun-dried tomatoes add a richness to the flavor as well as protein, fiber, and iron to the dish. Sun-dried tomatoes are also high in antioxidants and part of a heart-healthy diet.

¼ CUP LIGHT MAYONNAISE

2 TABLESPOONS CHOPPED SUN-DRIED TOMATOES

2 TABLESPOONS FRESHLY GRATED PARMESAN CHEESE

1 TEASPOON FRESHLY SQUEEZED LEMON JUICE

1 TEASPOON OLIVE OIL

4 EGGS

1 LARGE TOMATO, CUT INTO 8 THIN SLICES

½ CUP CHOPPED ARUGULA

FOUR ½-INCH-THICK SLICES CRUSTY FRENCH OR ITALIAN BREAD

FRESHLY GROUND PEPPER

1. In a small bowl, stir together the mayonnaise, sun-dried tomatoes, Parmesan cheese, and lemon juice until combined. Set aside.

2. In a large skillet over medium-high heat, heat the oil.

3. Crack the eggs into the skillet and use a spatula to break the yolks.

4. Cook the eggs for 4 minutes, or until set and remove the skillet from the heat.

5. Spread the mayonnaise mixture onto each piece of bread, and top with 2 slices of tomato and arugula.

6. Place the eggs on the arugula and season with salt and pepper.

7. Serve immediately.

Buttery Asparagus with Eggs

MAKES 4 SERVINGS

Prep time: 10 minutes
Cook time: 20 minutes

Serve this decadent dish as an appetizer or side. It is a wonderful and delicious way to get asparagus into your diet. Asparagus is high in many nutrients such as folic acid, beta-carotene, vitamin C, and fiber.

. . . .

Chef's Tip: *Look for pencil-width asparagus for this dish and be sure to trim the ends. An easy way to remove the woody ends is to bend the asparagus towards the end of the stalk. It will usually snap right where the woody part and tender part merge.*

. . . .

½ CUP BUTTER
4 HARD-BOILED EGGS (PAGE 35), PEELED
32 ASPARAGUS SPEARS, WOODY ENDS TRIMMED
SEA SALT AND FRESHLY GROUND PEPPER

1. In a medium heavy bottomed saucepan over low heat, melt the butter slowly.

2. Remove the saucepan from the heat and let stand for 5 minutes.

3. Carefully skim the foam from the top of the melted butter. Slowly pour the clear yellow butter into a container leaving the milky solids in the bottom of the saucepan. Discard the milky solids and set clarified butter aside.

4. With a box grater, grate the eggs into a medium bowl.

5. In a medium saucepan add enough water to fill halfway up the sides. Bring the water to a boil over high heat.

6. Add the asparagus and cook until crisp-tender, about 2 minutes.

continued ▶

7. Drain the asparagus and arrange on a serving plate in a single layer.

8. Top the asparagus with the grated egg and drizzle with clarified butter.

9. Season with salt and pepper.

10. Serve immediately.

Potato and Pepper Stew

MAKES 4 SERVINGS

Prep time: 15 minutes
Cook time: 30 minutes

You might want to try this hearty stew as a satisfying stick-to-the-ribs dinner after an active day outside, especially when the weather is cold. This stew can be made in a slow cooker for a ready-made meal. Combine everything in the slow cooker and cook for about 6 hours on low heat. Increase the chicken broth to 2½ cups and cook the eggs just before serving.

1 TABLESPOON OLIVE OIL
1 LARGE SWEET ONION, HALVED AND THINLY SLICED
3 TEASPOONS MINCED GARLIC
2 RED BELL PEPPERS, SEEDED AND DICED
1 YELLOW BELL PEPPER, SEEDED AND DICED
1 GREEN BELL PEPPER, SEEDED AND DICED
4 HOT ITALIAN SAUSAGE LINKS, COOKED AND CUBED
3 LARGE POTATOES, PEELED AND DICED
2 CUPS LOW-SODIUM CHICKEN BROTH
SEA SALT AND FRESHLY GROUND PEPPER
4 EGGS
¼ CUP CHOPPED FRESH PARSLEY

1. In a large skillet over medium-high heat, heat 1½ teaspoons of the oil. Sauté the onion, garlic, and peppers for 2 minutes.

2. Add the sausage and cook for 5 to 8 more minutes, or until the vegetables are tender.

3. Add the potatoes and the chicken broth.

4. Bring to a boil over medium-high heat. Cover, reduce the heat and simmer for 15 minutes, or until the potatoes are tender.

5. Remove the skillet from the heat and season with salt and pepper. Set aside.

6. In a large skillet over medium-high heat, heat the remaining oil. Add the eggs and cook for 4 minutes, or to desired doneness.

7. Divide the stew evenly among 4 serving bowls. Top each serving with an egg.

8. Sprinkle with parsley just before serving.

Eggs Poached in Curry Spices

Prep time: 5 minutes
Cook time: 4 minutes

Curry spices and eggs are a match made in heaven, and the eggs in this recipe soak up the curry flavor and beautiful yellow color for a wonderful result. The combination of spices can be adjusted to suit your taste. To save time, stir 2 tablespoons of prepared curry paste into your poaching water in place of the dried seasonings.

Timesaving Tip: *Mix together the spices ahead of time and store in a sealed container out of direct sunlight until you are ready to use them. The exotic blend of spices can be doubled. Just measure out 3 teaspoons to add to the poaching liquid for this recipe and save the rest for another dish.*

6 CUPS WATER
1 TEASPOON WHITE VINEGAR
1 TEASPOON CURRY POWDER
1 TEASPOON GROUND CORIANDER
½ TEASPOON TURMERIC
¼ TEASPOON GROUND CUMIN
PINCH OF CARDAMOM
PINCH OF SEA SALT
PINCH OF FRESHLY GROUND PEPPER
4 EGGS
2 ENGLISH MUFFINS, HALVED AND TOASTED

1. In a medium saucepan over medium-high heat, bring the water, vinegar, and spices to a boil.

2. Reduce the heat to medium-low and maintain a gentle simmer.

3. Break 1 egg into a small bowl. Gently pour the egg into the water.

4. Repeat the process with the remaining 3 eggs.

5. Cook the eggs in the simmering water for 3 to 5 minutes or to desired doneness.

6. Remove the eggs with a slotted spoon and drain well on paper towels.

7. Serve immediately on toasted English muffins.

Muffuletta Sandwich

MAKES 6 SERVINGS

Prep time: 15 minutes

Muffuletta sandwiches can be traced back to the French quarter in New Orleans. The traditional sandwich does not include egg, but it is a nice addition with the ingredients in this recipe. Try prosciutto or Parma ham in place of the turkey for a truly authentic sandwich, if you'd like.

ONE 10-INCH ROUND ITALIAN BREAD LOAF

3 TEASPOONS MAYONNAISE (PAGE 46 OR STORE-BOUGHT)

2 TEASPOONS PREPARED BASIL PESTO

2 CUPS THINLY SLICED SPINACH OR ARUGULA

8 HARD-BOILED EGGS (PAGE 35), SLICED

1 LARGE TOMATO, THINLY SLICED

½ SMALL RED ONION, THINLY SLICED

½ CUP SLICED BLACK OLIVES

½ CUP GRATED MOZZARELLA CHEESE

6 THIN SLICES DELI-ROASTED TURKEY BREAST

1. Cut off the top third of the bread and set aside.

2. Remove all but 1 inch of the bread inside to form a bread bowl. Reserve the scooped out portion for another use.

3. In a small bowl, combine the mayonnaise and pesto. Spread the mixture evenly on the insides of the bread bowl.

4. Layer the spinach, eggs, tomato, onion, olives, cheese, and turkey into the bread bowl.

5. Cover with the reserved bread loaf top.

6. Wrap the sandwich tightly with plastic wrap. Put a large plate or cast-iron skillet over the sandwich, and distribute a few heavy objects (such as cans of food) evenly on the plate or skillet.

7. Refrigerate for at least 4 hours.

8. Cut the sandwich into 6 wedges before serving.

Caprese Poached Eggs

MAKES 2 SERVINGS

Prep time: 5 minutes
Cook time: 10 minutes

This simple yet filling lunch or breakfast dish is inspired by Insalata Caprese and has English muffins and eggs added to the traditional salad components of basil, tomatoes, and fresh mozzarella. Look for fresh mozzarella from your local deli or gourmet store for the tastiest results.

1 TABLESPOON WHITE VINEGAR
4 EGGS
2 ENGLISH MUFFINS, HALVED
4 TEASPOONS PREPARED BASIL PESTO
1 LARGE TOMATO, CUT INTO 4 SLICES
4 SLICES FRESH MOZZARELLA CHEESE
FRESHLY GROUND PEPPER

1. Preheat the broiler to high.

2. Heat a large saucepan with 3 to 4 inches of water and the vinegar over high heat. Bring to a boil.

3. Reduce the heat to medium-low and maintain a gently simmer.

4. Break 1 egg into a small bowl. Gently pour the egg into the water.

5. Repeat the process with the remaining 3 eggs.

6. Cook the eggs in the simmering water 3 to 5 minutes or to desired doneness.

7. Remove the eggs with a slotted spoon and drain well on paper towels.

8. Spread the pesto onto each English muffin half. Top with tomato slices and mozzarella slices. Arrange the muffins on a baking sheet.

9. Broil for 30 seconds or until the cheese is bubbly and melted.

10. Remove from the oven and top each English muffin half with a poached egg.

11. Season with pepper and serve immediately.

CHAPTER NINE

Omelets, Frittatas, and Scrambles

Tomato Egg White Omelet

MAKES 2 SERVINGS

Prep time: 5 minutes
Cook time: 10 minutes

Egg white omelets are usually associated with weight loss diets and healthy eating because they are lower in fat and cholesterol than whole egg omelets. This can be appropriate for some diets to address issues like heart disease and cancer. Because this is an incredibly quick recipe, there is no reason to skip a healthy breakfast.

Chef's Tip: *One common issue with cooking egg whites is that they stick to the pan and create a mess. The best way to eliminate this problem is to preheat your pan well and to coat it liberally with olive oil cooking spray.*

2 TABLESPOONS OLIVE OIL

2 MEDIUM TOMATOES, FINELY CHOPPED

1 CUP THINLY SLICED SPINACH

2 GREEN ONIONS, CHOPPED

SEA SALT AND FRESHLY GROUND PEPPER

6 EGG WHITES

3 TEASPOONS WATER

OLIVE OIL COOKING SPRAY

1. In a large nonstick skillet over medium-high heat, heat the oil.

2. Add the tomatoes, spinach, and green onions.

3. Sauté for 2 to 3 minutes, or until the spinach is wilted.

4. Season with salt and pepper and remove the skillet from the heat. Set aside, cover, and keep warm. Wipe the skillet with a paper towel to clean.

5. In a medium bowl, whisk the egg whites and the water until frothy.

6. Heat the skillet to medium heat and coat with cooking spray.

7. Add the egg whites and cook until set, about 1½ to 2 minutes, swirling the pan and lifting the edges to allow the uncooked egg to run underneath the cooked egg white.

8. Spoon the spinach mixture onto the omelet. Fold the omelet in half and slide it onto a serving plate.

9. Cut the omelet in half and serve immediately.

California Omelet

Prep time: 5 minutes
Cook time: 10 minutes

You will be reminded of miles of sunny, sandy beaches and days spent in the ocean when you dig in to this healthy fresh-tasting omelet. The flavors are clean, and the fresh herbs provide gorgeous flecks of deep green in the fluffy egg. Make sure your avocado is nice and ripe by gently pressing into the stem end with your fingertip. If your avocado is still a bit green, place it in a paper bag with a ripe banana overnight and it should be soft and perfect by morning.

8 EGGS
2 TABLESPOONS 2 PERCENT MILK
1 TABLESPOON CHOPPED FRESH PARSLEY
1 TEASPOON CHOPPED FRESH BASIL
1 TEASPOON CHOPPED FRESH OREGANO
PINCH OF SEA SALT
PINCH OF FRESHLY GROUND PEPPER
OLIVE OIL COOKING SPRAY
1 SMALL PLUM TOMATO, DICED
1 GREEN ONION, CHOPPED
1 SMALL RIPE AVOCADO, PITTED, PEELED, AND SLICED
½ CUP GRATED MONTEREY JACK CHEESE

1. Preheat the broiler to high.

2. In a medium bowl, whisk together the eggs, milk, parsley, basil, oregano, salt, and pepper.

3. Put an oven-safe skillet over medium-high heat and coat lightly with cooking spray.

4. Pour the egg mixture into the skillet and swirl the pan lightly.

5. As the egg cooks, lift the edges of the to allow the uncooked egg to flow underneath.

6. Cook about 5 minutes, until the eggs are almost set. Remove the skillet from the heat.

7. Sprinkle the tomato over the omelet and arrange the green onion and avocado slices over the tomato.

8. Sprinkle evenly with the cheese and broil until the cheese is melted and the eggs are set.

9. Remove the skillet from the oven and fold the omelet in half.

10. Cut the omelet into 4 wedges before serving.

Mushroom and Pepper Frittata

MAKES 8 SERVINGS

Prep time: 15 minutes
Cook time: 45 minutes

There might be some confusion about the difference between this flat Italian egg dish and its fluffy French cousin, the omelet. Frittatas are traditionally cooked with all the ingredients mixed together in oven-safe skillets. After a brief moment on the stovetop, frittatas are finished in the oven. Traditional omelets are created on the stovetop and are folded over an assortment of delicious ingredients.

. . . .

Timesaving Tip: *Frittatas can actually improve in taste after a few hours either chilled or at room temperature. To save time, make this entire recipe in advance and serve it with a simple green salad for a light supper.*

. . . .

OLIVE OIL COOKING SPRAY
2 TABLESPOONS BUTTER
1 SMALL SWEET ONION, FINELY CHOPPED
1 TEASPOON MINCED GARLIC
2 CUPS SLICED BUTTON OR CREMINI MUSHROOMS
2 RED BELL PEPPERS, SEEDED AND DICED
¼ CUP CHOPPED FRESH PARSLEY
8 EGGS
1 CUP 2 PERCENT MILK
1½ CUPS GRATED SHARP CHEDDAR CHEESE
½ TEASPOON SEA SALT
¼ TEASPOON FRESHLY GROUND PEPPER

1. Preheat the oven to 350°F.

2. Coat a 9-by-13-inch baking dish with olive oil spray and set aside.

3. In a large skillet over medium-high heat, melt the butter.

4. Add the onion, garlic, and mushrooms and sauté until softened, about 5 minutes.

5. Add the red peppers and sauté for 5 minutes, or until the liquid in the skillet is evaporated.

6. Remove the skillet from the heat and stir in the parsley.

7. In a large bowl, whisk together the eggs, vegetables, milk, cheese, salt, and pepper.

8. Pour the mixture into the prepared baking dish and bake for 30 minutes or until set. Let the frittata stand 5 to 10 minutes before serving.

Speedy Potato and Ham Frittata

MAKES 4 SERVINGS

Prep time: 15 minutes
Cook time: 10 minutes

This frittata has all of the ingredients found in a nice hearty country breakfast in one handy dish! For an interesting flavor twist, try a maple-cured ham or find Canadian peameal bacon in place of the lean ham in the recipe. If you use peameal bacon, cook it ahead of time.

. . . .

Timesaving Tip: *For speedy brunch or breakfast gatherings, prepare this dish the night before and refrigerate it, uncooked, until the next morning. The morning of the get-together, uncover the frittata and bake it directly from the fridge in a 350°F oven for 35 minutes.*

. . . .

1 TEASPOON OLIVE OIL

1 SMALL SWEET ONION, CHOPPED

1 TEASPOON MINCED GARLIC

2 CUPS COOKED DICED POTATOES

6 EGGS

¾ CUP DICED LEAN HAM

1 CUP GRATED SHARP CHEDDAR CHEESE

DASH OF SEA SALT

DASH OF FRESHLY GROUND PEPPER

1 TEASPOON CHOPPED FRESH PARSLEY

1. Preheat the broiler to high.

2. In large oven-safe nonstick skillet over medium-high heat, heat the oil. Add the onion and the garlic and sauté for 3 minutes, or until tender.

3. Add the potatoes and sauté 2 to 3 more minutes.

4. In a medium bowl, whisk together the eggs, ham, ½ cup of the cheese, salt, and pepper.

5. Add the egg mixture to the skillet and reduce the heat to medium.

6. Cook for about 5 minutes, until the bottom of the frittata is set and browned, lifting the edges of the cooked egg to allow uncooked egg to flow underneath.

7. Sprinkle the remaining cheese over the top of the frittata and broil until the mixture is completely set and the cheese is melted, about 1 to 2 minutes.

8. Cut the frittata into wedges and sprinkle with parsley.

Sun-Dried Tomato and Broccoli Frittata

MAKES 6 SERVINGS

Prep time: 15 minutes
Cook time: 15 minutes

Broccoli is a great addition to frittatas because it holds up well in any cooking application, even baked in the oven. Broccoli has many health benefits, including lowering cholesterol, detoxing the body, and reducing the risk of cancer and cardiovascular disease. It is a wonderful source of fiber, vitamin C, and vitamin K.

10 LARGE EGGS
½ CUP 2 PERCENT MILK
1 TEASPOON DRIED OREGANO
1 TEASPOON DRIED BASIL
DASH OF SEA SALT
DASH OF FRESHLY GROUND PEPPER
2 CUPS COOKED BROCCOLI, CHOPPED
10 SUN-DRIED TOMATOES, CHOPPED
1 TEASPOON OLIVE OIL
½ CUP GRATED SHARP CHEDDAR CHEESE

1. Preheat the broiler to high.

2. In a large bowl, whisk together the eggs, milk, oregano, basil, salt, and pepper until thoroughly combined.

3. Whisk in the broccoli and sun-dried tomatoes.

4. Put a large oven-safe skillet over medium heat and add the olive oil.

5. Add the egg mixture to the skillet.

6. Cook for about 10 minutes, until the frittata is almost set, lifting the edges of the cooked egg to allow the uncooked egg to flow underneath.

7. Remove the skillet from the heat and sprinkle the top of the frittata with the cheese.

8. Broil the frittata until the cheese is melted and the frittata is cooked through, about 2 minutes.

9. Cut the frittata into wedges before serving.

Spinach Frittata

MAKES 6 SERVINGS

Prep time: 15 minutes
Cook time: 30 minutes

This frittata has a lovely rich taste and creamy texture because it uses sour cream instead of milk. If you are a vegetarian, make sure to read the nutrition labels when buying commercial sour cream. It can contain ingredients such as gelatin and rennet, which are animal products.

OLIVE OIL COOKING SPRAY

4 CUPS COOKED DICED POTATOES

2 CUPS CHOPPED SPINACH

1 RED BELL PEPPER, SEEDED AND DICED

1 YELLOW BELL PEPPER, SEEDED AND DICED

2 GREEN ONIONS, CHOPPED

8 EGGS, BEATEN

1 CUP SOUR CREAM

1 TABLESPOON CHOPPED FRESH BASIL

1 TABLESPOON CHOPPED FRESH DILL

DASH OF SEA SALT

DASH OF FRESHLY GROUND PEPPER

1. Preheat the oven to 350°F.

2. Coat a 9-by-13-inch baking dish with cooking spray; set aside.

3. In a large bowl, stir together all the ingredients until thoroughly combined.

4. Pour the mixture into the prepared baking dish and bake for 30 minutes, or until a knife inserted in the center comes out clean.

Egg and Vegetable Casserole

MAKES 6 SERVINGS

Prep time: 15 minutes
Cook time: 25 minutes

This complex dish is like an egg lasagna but is much easier to put together. It is full of vegetables, Italian herbs, and rich cheese. Substitute ricotta cheese for the cottage cheese, if you'd like. The finished dish will be less creamy.

12 EGGS
1 CUP 2 PERCENT COTTAGE CHEESE
1 TEASPOON DRIED THYME
1 TEASPOON DRIED OREGANO
1 TEASPOON DRIED BASIL
PINCH OF SEA SALT
PINCH FRESHLY GROUND PEPPER
1 CUP COOKED SLICED CARROTS
1 CUP COOKED BROCCOLI FLORETS
1 CUP COOKED HALVED GREEN BEANS
½ RED BELL PEPPER, SEEDED AND DICED
1 GREEN ONION, CHOPPED
½ CUP GRATED SWISS CHEESE

1. Preheat the oven to 350°F.

2. Lightly coat a 9-by-13-inch baking dish with cooking spray; set aside.

3. In a large bowl, whisk together the eggs, cottage cheese, herbs, salt, and pepper.

4. Pour half of the egg mixture into the prepared dish.

5. Spread the vegetables and the cheese over the top of the egg mixture.

6. Pour the remaining egg mixture over the vegetables and the cheese.

7. Bake the casserole for 20 to 25 minutes or until a knife inserted near the center comes out clean.

Ham, Mushroom, and Potato Bread Casserole

MAKES 4 SERVINGS

Prep time: 15 minutes
Cook time: 30 minutes

This breakfast casserole is a savory bread pudding, and the flavor can be tweaked easily by using different types of bread. For a slightly sweeter version, try raisin bread or brioche. Or, for a variety in texture, use a multigrain loaf as the base. If you are not counting calories and want a decadent brunch dish, try croissants instead of bread.

COOKING SPRAY
FOUR ½-INCH-THICK SLICES BREAD, CUT INTO QUARTERS
6 EGGS
1¼ CUPS 2 PERCENT MILK
THREE ¼-INCH-THICK SLICES SMOKED HAM, DICED
½ CUP SLICED BUTTON OR CREMINI MUSHROOMS
½ CUP GRATED SHARP CHEDDAR CHEESE
½ CUP COOKED DICED POTATOES

1. Preheat the oven to 350°F.

2. Coat an 8-inch square baking dish with cooking spray and arrange the bread pieces to cover the bottom completely.

3. In a medium bowl, whisk together the eggs, milk, ham, mushrooms, and ¼ cup of the cheese.

4. Pour the mixture over the bread in the baking dish and sprinkle with the potatoes and the remaining cheese.

5. Bake the casserole for about 30 minutes or until the eggs are set and the casserole is lightly browned.

Italian Sausage Baked Egg Casserole

MAKES 6 SERVINGS

Prep time: 5 minutes
Cook time: 25 minutes

Casseroles are a wonderful and delicious way to use up all of the ingredients in your fridge. This dish would also be very good with chopped artichoke hearts, grated carrot, and even sautéed fennel. Try hot Italian sausage or chorizo instead of the mild version here if you love spicy foods.

· ·

Chef's Tip: *If you don't have evaporated milk, you can make your own by gently simmering whole milk until it is about half the original volume. This takes several hours, and be careful not boil it or you can end up with scorched milk solids on the bottom of your pot.*

· ·

OLIVE OIL COOKING SPRAY

2 MILD ITALIAN SAUSAGE LINKS, CASINGS REMOVED

½ SMALL SWEET ONION, CHOPPED

2 TEASPOONS MINCED GARLIC

1 RED BELL PEPPER, SEEDED AND DICED

10 SUN-DRIED TOMATOES, CHOPPED

2 TABLESPOONS CHOPPED FRESH BASIL

1 CUP GRATED MOZZARELLA CHEESE

8 EGGS

ONE 12-OUNCE CAN EVAPORATED MILK

2 TABLESPOONS CHOPPED FRESH PARSLEY

1. Preheat the oven to 375°F.

2. Coat six 10-ounce ramekins lightly with cooking spray; set aside.

3. In a medium skillet coated with cooking spray over medium-high heat, cook the sausage for 4 minutes or until browned. Drain the sausage.

4. Wipe the skillet clean and return the sausage to the skillet. Add the onion, garlic, and red bell pepper. Sauté for about 3 minutes, or until the vegetables are softened.

5. Add the sun-dried tomatoes and basil and sauté for 1 more minute.

6. Divide the sausage mixture evenly among the prepared ramekins.

7. Sprinkle about 2 tablespoons of the cheese over the sausage in each ramekin.

8. In a large bowl, whisk together the eggs and evaporated milk.

9. Pour the egg mixture evenly into the ramekins over the cheese and sausage mixture.

10. Sprinkle the remaining cheese and parsley over the egg mixture.

11. Bake the casseroles for about 15 minutes or until a knife inserted into the center comes out clean.

Egg Tacos

MAKES 4 SERVINGS

Prep time: 15 minutes
Cook time: 5 minutes

Most people are familiar with egg wraps, but hard taco shells work just as well to hold this colorful egg mixture. For best results, be sure to warm the taco shells so that they are more flexible and do not shatter when you bite into them. Hard taco shells began appearing in Mexican American cookbooks as early as 1914.

4 HARD TACO SHELLS

4 EGGS

¼ CUP 2 PERCENT MILK

1 TEASPOON CHILI POWDER

1 TEASPOON OLIVE OIL

1 MEDIUM TOMATO, FINELY CHOPPED

1 CUP SHREDDED LETTUCE

½ CUP GRATED SHARP CHEDDAR CHEESE

¼ CUP FRESH SALSA

1. Preheat the oven to 250°F.

2. Wrap the taco shells in a clean kitchen towel and place in the oven to warm.

3. In a small bowl, whisk together the eggs, milk, and chili powder.

4. Put a small skillet over medium-high heat and add the oil.

5. Pour the egg mixture into the skillet and use a spatula to scramble the eggs until they are fluffy, cooked through, and dry.

6. Divide the scrambled eggs evenly among the warmed taco shells.

7. Top each taco with tomato, lettuce, cheese, and salsa.

8. Serve immediately.

Scrambled Egg Wrap

MAKES 2 SERVINGS

Prep time: 5 minutes
Cook time: 2 minutes

For a quick grab-and-run-out-the-door meal, this simple wrap fits the bill. In under ten minutes, you can have a protein- and antioxidant-packed meal to help fuel your body without creating blood sugar spikes or filling you up too much. You can even cook the eggs in the microwave to make the preparation even faster. Simply pour the beaten eggs into a ramekin or dish and microwave about 1½ minutes, then spoon the cooked egg into your wrap.

3 EGGS

PINCH OF SEA SALT

DASH OF FRESHLY GROUND PEPPER

1 TEASPOON OLIVE OIL

TWO 6-INCH FLOUR TORTILLAS

2 TABLESPOONS MAYONNAISE (PAGE 46 OR STORE-BOUGHT)

2 SLICES SMOKED DELI TURKEY BREAST

2 LARGE LETTUCE LEAVES

1 SMALL TOMATO, DICED

1. In a small bowl, whisk together the eggs, salt, and pepper.

2. In a small nonstick skillet over medium heat, heat the oil. Add the eggs.

3. Scramble the eggs until cooked through but not dry. Remove the skillet from the heat.

4. Place the tortillas on a clean work surface and spread each with 1 tablespoon of mayonnaise.

5. Top each tortilla with 1 slice of turkey, 1 lettuce leaf, and half the scrambled eggs.

6. Top the egg with the chopped tomato and roll up the tortillas.

7. Serve immediately.

Smoked Chicken and Egg Pitas

Prep time: 10 minutes
Cook time: 10 minutes

Pita pockets make handy sandwiches perfect for picnics and other outdoor events. Pita bread, a staple in Middle Eastern cuisine, is usually made from very few ingredients, and the combination of thin rolling, high heat, and the water turning to steam to produce hyperactive yeast creates the pocket in the bread. If you have a very hot oven, you can even try to make pita bread at home.

1 TEASPOON OLIVE OIL

1 GREEN ONION, CHOPPED

1 SMALL RED BELL PEPPER, SEEDED AND FINELY CHOPPED

6 EGGS, BEATEN

½ CUP CHOPPED SMOKED CHICKEN

¼ CUP GOAT CHEESE, CRUMBLED

2 TABLESPOONS DIJON MUSTARD

2 WHOLE-WHEAT PITA BREADS, HALVED

4 LARGE BOSTON OR BIBB LETTUCE LEAVES

1. In a large nonstick skillet over medium heat, heat the oil.

2. Add the green onion and red bell pepper and cook until softened, about 4 minutes.

3. Add the eggs, chicken, and cheese to the skillet.

4. Scramble the egg mixture gently to form fluffy curds and cook for 5 minutes, or until the egg is cooked through.

5. Remove the skillet from the heat.

6. Spread the Dijon mustard inside each pita half.

7. Line each pita with lettuce.

8. Spoon the scrambled egg mixture evenly into each pita.

9. Serve immediately.

Bacon and Corn Scrambled Eggs

MAKES 4 SERVINGS

Prep time: 5 minutes
Cook time: 15 minutes

The combination of bacon and corn is a familiar one, especially to people in the southern United States. Cornbread studded with bacon and creamy corn chowders topped with salty crumbled bacon are traditional offerings at most tables. You can use fresh or frozen corn in this recipe but canned works just as well, as long as it doesn't contain salt.

8 EGGS
6 SLICES BACON, COOKED AND CRUMBLED
1 CUP CANNED NO-SALT-ADDED CORN KERNELS
1 GREEN ONION, CHOPPED
PINCH OF FRESHLY GROUND PEPPER
OLIVE OIL COOKING SPRAY

1. In a large bowl, whisk together the eggs, bacon, corn, green onion, and pepper.

2. In a large skillet coated with cooking spray over medium-high heat, add the egg mixture.

3. Scramble the eggs until they form large curds and there is no visible liquid.

4. Serve immediately.

Vegetable Fried Rice

MAKES 4 SERVINGS

Prep time: 10 minutes
Cook time: 10 minutes

Fried rice is often used as a side dish in Asian-themed restaurants, but this makes a nice main course as well. The trick to great fried rice is to scramble the eggs in the center of the rice on the skillet and stir the cooked egg into the rice as you go. Having larger curds of cooked egg adds a nice texture contrast, so don't over-mix the dish while frying.

4 EGGS
2 TEASPOONS LOW-SODIUM SOY SAUCE
1 TABLESPOON OLIVE OIL
4 GREEN ONIONS, SLICED DIAGONALLY
2 STALKS CELERY, FINELY DICED
1 RED BELL PEPPER, SEEDED AND CHOPPED
1 SMALL CARROT, PEELED AND FINELY DICED
½ TEASPOON MINCED GARLIC
¼ TEASPOON GROUND GINGER
3 CUPS COOKED LONG-GRAIN RICE

1. In a small bowl, whisk together the eggs and soy sauce; set aside.

2. In a large skillet or wok over medium-high heat, heat the oil.

3. Add the green onions, celery, red pepper, carrot, and garlic, and sauté until the vegetables are softened, about 3 minutes.

4. Stir in the ginger.

5. Add the rice and stir until thoroughly combined. Make a well in the center of the rice mixture.

6. Pour the egg mixture into the well and scramble the until the egg is cooked. Stir the egg into the rice until thoroughly combined.

7. Remove the skillet from the heat.

8. Serve immediately.

CHAPTER TEN

Baked Egg Dishes: Quiches, Pies, Soufflés, and Custards

Cheese Custard

Prep time: 15 minutes
Cook time: 20 minutes

Custards are often thought of as sweet dishes, but savory custards also have a long culinary history. Quiches are actually savory custards baked in flaky pie crusts. Baked custards, like this one, became quite popular after the 17th century because it was possible to create the water bath needed to help set the dish. As ovens became more modern so did the techniques used to create these delicate egg dishes.

Chef's Tip: *Never boil your custard mixture, or you run the risk of curdling the eggs or overcooking them, which will ruin the texture and taste.*

2 CUPS WHOLE MILK
½ CUP GRATED GRUYÈRE CHEESE
2 EGGS
2 EGG YOLKS
¼ TEASPOON CHOPPED FRESH THYME
PINCH OF SEA SALT
PINCH OF FRESHLY GROUND BLACK PEPPER
PINCH OF CAYENNE PEPPER

1. Preheat the oven to 350°F.

2. Place four 4-ounce ramekins in a 9-inch square baking pan and set aside.

3. In a small saucepan, heat the milk until bubbles form around the edges. Do not boil.

4. Whisk in the cheese and stir until it is melted; set aside.

5. In a large bowl, whisk together the eggs, egg yolks, thyme, salt, black pepper, and cayenne pepper until thoroughly combined.

6. While whisking constantly, slowly add the milk mixture to the egg mixture in a slow, steady stream.

7. Pour the egg mixture evenly into the ramekins.

8. Pour hot water into the baking pan about halfway up the sides of the ramekins.

9. Bake the custards for about 20 minutes or until the centers are set.

10. Remove the custards from the oven, and carefully remove the ramekins from the water bath.

11. Let the custards stand at room temperature until they are warm.

Baked Herb Custard

MAKES 6 SERVINGS

Prep time: 10 minutes
Cook time: 35 minutes

Almost all herbs go very nicely with the mild creaminess of this baked custard dish. If you have a favorite herb like tarragon or thyme, substitute it for the parsley and chives, but adjusting the amount according to the strength of the herb's flavor. For example, if using thyme instead of parsley, use only 1 or 2 tablespoons because it has a more powerful impact than parsley. Use your best judgment and experiment to find exactly the right combination.

. . . .

Chef's Tip: *Never substitute egg yolks for whole eggs in a set custard recipe; the egg whites are necessary for the custard to set. The whites contain albumen, which forms the gel or matrix structure in the set custard. For a a very firm custard, add an extra egg white to your recipe.*

. . . .

¾ CUP 2 PERCENT MILK
½ CUP WHIPPING CREAM
1 TEASPOON MINCED GARLIC
4 EGGS
¼ CUP CHOPPED FRESH PARSLEY
2 TABLESPOONS CHOPPED FRESH CHIVES
SEA SALT AND FRESHLY GROUND PEPPER

1. Preheat the oven to 300°F.

2. Place six 6-ounce ramekins in a large baking dish; set aside.

3. In a medium saucepan over medium-high heat, combine the milk, whipping cream, and garlic.

4. Heat the milk until bubbles form around the edges. Do not boil. Remove the pan from the heat.

5. In a large bowl, beat the eggs. While whisking constantly, slowly add the hot milk mixture to the eggs in a slow, steady stream.

6. Whisk in the herbs and season with salt and pepper.

7. Pour the egg mixture evenly into the ramekins.

8. Pour hot water into the baking pan about halfway up the sides of the ramekins.

9. Bake the custards for about 30 minutes or until the centers are set.

10. Remove the custards from the oven, and carefully remove the ramekins from the water bath.

11. Serve immediately or let stand until warm.

Pumpkin Soufflé

MAKES 4 SERVINGS

Prep time: 15 minutes
Cook time: 15 minutes

This recipe takes a favorite dessert, pumpkin pie, and creates an even more luscious version. You can easily serve this soufflé as a side dish or first course because it is not overly sweet. Make sure you purchase plain cooked pumpkin instead of pie filling or this dish will be too sweet.

BUTTER
½ CUP GRANULATED SUGAR, PLUS MORE FOR DUSTING
6 EGGS, SEPARATED AND AT ROOM TEMPERATURE
1 TEASPOON CREAM OF TARTAR
½ CUP CANNED PUMPKIN
¼ TEASPOON GROUND CINNAMON
¼ TEASPOON GROUND GINGER
PINCH OF GROUND CLOVES
PINCH OF GROUND NUTMEG

1. Preheat the oven to 375°F.

2. Use the butter to grease the bottoms and sides of four 8-ounce soufflé dishes; dust them thoroughly with sugar.

3. Place the dishes in a 9-by-13-inch baking pan. Set aside.

4. In a large stainless steel bowl, whisk the egg whites and cream of tartar until foamy.

5. While whisking, add the remaining ½ cup sugar, 2 tablespoons at a time, beating after each addition until the sugar is dissolved.

6. Continue beating until the egg whites are glossy and form stiff peaks.

7. In a separate bowl, beat the egg yolks until they are very thick and pale yellow. Fold the pumpkin and spices into the egg yolks until thoroughly blended.

8. Gently fold the pumpkin mixture into the whipped egg whites until combined. Spoon the batter evenly into the soufflé dishes.

9. Place the baking pan in the middle of the oven. Pour hot water into the baking pan about halfway up the sides of the soufflé dishes.

10. Bake the soufflés 15 to 20 minutes or until they are puffed and lightly browned.

11. Serve immediately.

Farmhouse Baked Eggs

MAKES 4 SERVINGS

Prep time: 15 minutes
Cook time: 15 minutes

If you don't have any ramekins, you can actually cook these eggs in sturdy ceramic mugs as well. After they are cooked, let the mugs stand until the handles cool down enough to hold them. Then eat this tasty dish sitting on the porch or a cool deck with no plates to clean up later.

Timesaving Tip: *Prepare these eggs, without baking, the night before and place them, covered, on a baking sheet and store them in the refrigerator. Bake them straight from the refrigerator the next morning.*

10 NEW POTATOES, COOKED AND QUARTERED

4 SLICES SMOKED DELI TURKEY, CUT INTO ¼-INCH-THICK STRIPS

1 TABLESPOON OLIVE OIL

SEA SALT AND FRESHLY GROUND PEPPER

1 CUP CHILI SAUCE

8 EGGS

4 TEASPOONS CHOPPED FRESH PARSLEY

1. Preheat the oven to 375°F.

2. Place four 8-ounce ramekins on a large rimmed baking sheet; set aside.

3. In a small bowl, combine the potatoes, turkey, and oil.

4. Season with salt and pepper.

5. Divide the potato mixture evenly among the ramekins.

6. Top the potato mixture evenly with the chili sauce.

7. Crack 2 eggs into each ramekin over the chili sauce.

8. Bake for about 15 minutes. Sprinkle with parsley before serving.

Portuguese Baked Eggs

MAKES 6 SERVINGS

Prep time: 15 minutes
Cook time: 40 minutes

Red peppers are a very common ingredient in Portuguese cooking, mostly in the form of a prepared paste. The red peppers in this recipe are not in paste form, but they still add a lovely sweet taste and color to the finished dish. Garlic is also a staple Portuguese ingredient and it is used liberally in this sauce. For a more authentic stew, crush the garlic instead of mincing it for a more pronounced garlic flavor.

2 TABLESPOONS OLIVE OIL
4 TEASPOONS MINCED GARLIC
2 RED BELL PEPPERS, SEEDED AND THINLY SLICED
1 YELLOW BELL PEPPER, SEEDED AND THINLY SLICED
2 LARGE TOMATOES, CHOPPED
1 SMALL RED ONION, THINLY SLICED
4 TABLESPOONS CHOPPED FRESH BASIL
2 TABLESPOONS CHOPPED FRESH OREGANO
2 TABLESPOONS CHILI POWDER
SEA SALT AND FRESHLY GROUND PEPPER
6 TABLESPOONS RICOTTA CHEESE
6 EGGS
1 CUP GRATED SHARP CHEDDAR CHEESE
TOASTED BREAD SLICES

1. Preheat the oven to 400°F.

2. In a large skillet over medium-high heat, heat the oil.

3. Add the garlic, peppers, tomatoes, and onion and sauté for about 10 minutes, or until the vegetables are softened.

4. Add the basil, oregano, and chili powder.

5. Cook, stirring occasionally, for 10 minutes.

continued ▶

Portuguese Baked Eggs *continued* ▶

6. Season with salt and pepper.

7. Spoon the vegetable mixture into a 9-by-13-inch baking dish. Make 6 wells in the mixture with the back of a spoon.

8. Spoon 1 tablespoon of ricotta cheese into each well and crack 1 egg on top of the ricotta. Top with Cheddar cheese.

9. Bake until the eggs are almost set but the egg yolks are still runny, about 15 minutes.

10. Serve the baked eggs with the toasted bread slices.

Kitchen Sink Quiche

MAKES 8 SERVINGS

Prep time: 20 minutes
Cook time: 50 minutes

This is a full meal quiche rather than a delicate creation intended to be served at tea or for a ladies' luncheon. The prepared pie crust adds convenience, but use a homemade crust if you prefer.

ONE 9-INCH DEEP-DISH PIE CRUST
1 TABLESPOON OLIVE OIL
½ SMALL SWEET ONION, FINELY DICED
½ JALAPEÑO PEPPER, FINELY DICED
½ CUP SLICED BUTTON OR CREMINI MUSHROOMS
½ RED BELL PEPPER, SEEDED AND DICED
½ CUP DICED SMOKED HAM
½ CUP GRATED SHARP CHEDDAR CHEESE
4 EGGS
¾ CUP WHOLE MILK
½ CUP HEAVY CREAM
½ TEASPOON GROUND NUTMEG
PINCH OF SEA SALT
PINCH OF FRESHLY GROUND PEPPER

1. Preheat the oven to 400°F.

2. Line the pie crust with aluminum foil and fill it with dried beans.

3. Bake the crust until the edges are golden brown, about 15 minutes.

4. Remove the aluminum foil and the beans; let the crust cool.

5. Reduce the oven temperature to 350°F.

6. In a large skillet over medium-high heat, heat the oil. Add the onion, jalapeño pepper, mushrooms, and red bell pepper and sauté until the vegetables are softened, about 4 minutes.

continued ▶

7. Remove the skillet from the heat and stir in the ham.

8. In a medium bowl, whisk together the cheese, eggs, milk, cream, nutmeg, salt, and pepper.

9. Spoon the ham and vegetable mixture into the prepared pie crust and pour in the egg mixture.

10. Bake the quiche for 30 minutes or until a knife inserted in the center comes out clean.

11. Serve warm.

Gouda and Bacon Quiche

MAKES 8 SERVINGS

Prep time: 15 minutes
Cook time: 45 minutes

Gouda cheese is produced all around the world today but originated in a town in Holland of the same name. In its most basic version, this cheese is quite sweet because some of the milk sugars are removed early in its production for a less acidic finish. You may be surprised to find many types of Gouda cheese on the market— from the mild milky young cheeses to aged cheeses that are a deep caramel color. This cheese can be flavored with herbs, washed in beer, and even smoked. Try different types in this quiche until you find a favorite.

ONE 9-INCH DEEP-DISH PIE CRUST
6 SLICES BACON, CHOPPED
1 TEASPOON OLIVE OIL
½ SMALL SWEET ONION, CHOPPED
2 TEASPOONS MINCED GARLIC
¼ TEASPOON DRIED BASIL
DASH OF FRESHLY GROUND PEPPER
PINCH OF SALT
½ RED BELL PEPPER, SEEDED AND CHOPPED
1 GREEN ONION, CHOPPED
¾ CUP GRATED AGED GOUDA CHEESE
3 EGGS
¾ CUP 2 PERCENT MILK

1. Preheat the oven to 400°F.

2. Line the pie crust with aluminum foil and fill it with dried beans.

3. Bake the crust until the edges are golden brown, about 15 minutes.

4. Remove the aluminum foil and the beans; let the crust cool.

5. Reduce the oven temperature to 375°F.

6. In a large skillet over medium-high heat, sauté the chopped bacon until crisp, about 5 minutes.

continued ▶

7. Remove the bacon with a slotted spoon to paper towels to drain.

8. Wipe the skillet clean.

9. Add the olive oil to the skillet. Sauté the onion, garlic, basil, pepper, and salt about 5 minutes, or until the onion is softened.

10. Transfer the onion mixture to a bowl and add the bacon, red bell pepper, and green onion.

11. Sprinkle half of the cheese in the bottom of the cooled pie crust.

12. Spread the bacon mixture over the cheese.

13. In a small bowl, whisk together the eggs and the milk.

14. Pour the egg mixture over the bacon mixture and sprinkle with the remaining cheese.

15. Bake the quiche for about 30 minutes, or until a knife inserted in the center comes out clean.

16. Let the quiche cool for 10 minutes before serving.

Baked French Toast

MAKES 3 SERVINGS

Prep time: 10 minutes
Cook time: 30 minutes

Although called "French" toast, it's not certain if this dish was actually invented in France. In ancient Rome, for example, cooks used up their stale bread in this delicious manner, and cultures all over the world probably used similar methods to eliminate food waste.

2 TABLESPOONS MELTED BUTTER PLUS EXTRA FOR GREASING THE BAKING DISH

SIX ½-INCH-THICK SLICES WHOLE WHEAT-BREAD

1 TEASPOON GROUND CINNAMON

3 EGGS

½ CUP 2 PERCENT MILK

½ CUP MAPLE SYRUP

1 TEASPOON VANILLA EXTRACT

1. Preheat the oven to 350°F.

2. Grease a 9-by-13-inch baking dish.

3. Arrange the bread slices evenly in the dish.

4. Sprinkle the cinnamon over the bread.

5. In a medium bowl, whisk together the eggs, milk, maple syrup, melted butter, and vanilla until combined.

6. Pour the egg mixture evenly over the bread.

7. Bake the French toast for 30 minutes or until firm to the touch.

8. Serve warm.

Nested Eggs

MAKES 4 SERVINGS

Prep time: 10 minutes
Cook time: 30 minutes

This savory chicken stew is topped with perfect baked eggs.The stew is lightly flavored with parsley and celery leaves to allow the chicken to shine. Celery greens are not just packed with flavor; they also contain about five times the amount of calcium and magnesium as the stalks. The celery greens are also a great source of vitamin C, so always incorporate them in your recipes if you can.

2 TABLESPOONS OLIVE OIL

1 SMALL SWEET ONION, CHOPPED

2 STALKS CELERY WITH LEAVES, FINELY CHOPPED

1 LARGE POTATO, PEELED AND CUT INTO SMALL CUBES

3 TABLESPOONS CHOPPED FRESH PARSLEY

1 TEASPOON DRIED BASIL

1 TEASPOON DRIED THYME

SEA SALT AND FRESHLY GROUND PEPPER

1 CUP CUBED COOKED CHICKEN

½ CUP LOW-SODIUM CHICKEN BROTH

8 EGGS

1. Preheat the oven to 350°F.

2. In a large oven-safe nonstick skillet over medium heat, heat the oil. Add the onion and the celery and sauté until softened, about 3 minutes.

3. Add the potato and sauté about 5 minutes, stirring often, until lightly browned.

4. Stir in the parsley, basil, thyme, salt, pepper, and chicken. Cook, stirring occasionally, for about 3 minutes.

5. Add the broth and bring the mixture to a boil.

6. Transfer the skillet to the oven and bake for about 15 minutes, or until the potatoes are tender.

7. Remove the skillet from the oven. With a large spoon, make 8 deep wells in the potato mixture.

8. Crack 1 egg into each well and return the skillet to the oven. Bake for 6 more minutes, or until the eggs are set.

9. Serve immediately.

Bread and Cheese Soufflé

MAKES 6 SERVINGS

Prep time: 20 minutes
Cook time: 50 minutes

If you like bread puddings and are enchanted with soufflés, this dish is really the perfect choice for you. Be sure to leave the soufflé dish ungreased because the height achieved in this masterpiece is created when the soufflé batter clings to the sides of the dish as it rises. If you grease the pan the soufflé will not rise.

3 TABLESPOONS BUTTER
3 TABLESPOONS ALL-PURPOSE FLOUR
1 CUP 2 PERCENT MILK
6 EGGS, SEPARATED AND AT ROOM TEMPERATURE
1 CUP GRATED SHARP CHEDDAR CHEESE
½ TEASPOON DRY MUSTARD
DASH OF FRESHLY GROUND PEPPER
PINCH OF SEA SALT
1½ CUPS FRESH BREAD, CUBED

1. Preheat the oven to 300°F.

2. In a large saucepan over low heat, melt the butter.

3. Whisk the flour into the butter and cook, stirring constantly, for 1 minute.

4. Whisk in the milk and cook, stirring constantly, until thickened, about 4 minutes.

5. Remove the saucepan from the heat.

6. While whisking, add the egg yolks, 2 at a time, to the flour mixture.

7. Whisk in the cheese, mustard, pepper, and salt. Transfer the cheese mixture to large bowl and set aside.

8. In a medium bowl, beat the egg whites until stiff peaks form.

9. Gently fold the beaten egg whites into the cheese mixture. Gently stir in the bread cubes.

10. Spoon the batter into an ungreased 8-cup soufflé dish.

11. Bake the soufflé until it is puffed and golden brown, about 50 minutes.

12. Serve immediately.

CHAPTER ELEVEN

Vegetarian Entrées

APPLE OMELET

EGGY POTATO SKINS

SIMPLE SALSA VERDE EGGS

CAULIFLOWER EGG CURRY

RATATOUILLE WITH POACHED EGGS

VEGGIE SCRAMBLED EGGS

ROLLED OMELET WITH SPINACH

EGGS IN BELL PEPPERS

EASY EGG CURRY

EGGS BAKED IN TOMATOES

ASPARAGUS AND GOAT CHEESE QUICHE

ARUGULA AND FENNEL OMELETS

INDIVIDUAL CHILE CASSEROLES

TASTY SPINACH CAKES

EGG STIR-FRY

Apple Omelet

Prep time: 10 minutes
Cook time: 10 minutes

Before modern cooking methods and refrigeration, it was popular to serve the combination of cheese and fruit after a meal. Apples and cheese are a heavenly match and are delicious in this omelet. Try to find a good quality Cheddar at least two years old for the best results.

1 TABLESPOON BUTTER
1 MEDIUM APPLE, PEELED, CORED, AND THINLY SLICED
½ TEASPOON GROUND CINNAMON
DASH OF GROUND NUTMEG
1 TABLESPOON LIGHT BROWN SUGAR
5 EGGS
2 TABLESPOONS WATER
PINCH OF SALT
¼ CUP GRATED SHARP CHEDDAR CHEESE

1. In a medium nonstick skillet over medium-high heat, melt the butter.

2. Add the apple and sauté for about 3 minutes.

3. Add the cinnamon, nutmeg, and brown sugar; cook for 4 more minutes.

4. In a small bowl, whisk together the eggs, water, and salt.

5. Pour the egg mixture evenly over the apples in the skillet. Swirl the pan lightly.

6. As the egg cooks, lift the edges of the to allow the uncooked egg to flow underneath.

7. When the omelet is almost set, sprinkle the cheese over one half.

8. Fold the half of the omelet over the cheese and cook for 1 more minute.

9. Cut the omelet in half and serve warm.

Eggy Potato Skins

MAKES 4 SERVINGS

Prep time: 15 minutes
Cook time: 15 minutes

Potatoes make very handy containers for eggs, and this humble tuber is the most prolific crop in the world. Potatoes are an excellent source of vitamin C, vitamin B6, fiber, and potassium. Potatoes can help lower blood pressure, increase brain activity, and help reduce the risk of cardiovascular disease.

. . . .

Chef's Tip: *There are so many types of potatoes and it can be daunting to find the right one for baking. Choose potatoes without green sprouts or blemishes and those that haven't been prewashed—prewashing removes the dirt, and leaves them vulnerable to bacteria.*

. . . .

2 LARGE POTATOES, BAKED

4 EGGS

2 TABLESPOONS PLAIN GREEK YOGURT

1 GREEN ONION, CHOPPED

¾ CUP GRATED SHARP CHEDDAR CHEESE

SEA SALT AND FRESHLY GROUND PEPPER

1. Preheat the oven to 375°F.

2. Cut the potatoes in half lengthwise and carefully scoop out the flesh, leaving the skins intact.

3. In a small bowl, combine the cooked potato flesh, eggs, yogurt, green onion, and ½ cup of the cheese.

4. Season with salt and pepper.

5. Spoon the egg mixture evenly into the potato skins and sprinkle with the remaining cheese.

6. Bake the potatoes for about 15 minutes or until the cheese melts.

Simple Salsa Verde Eggs

MAKES 2 SERVINGS

Prep time: 5 minutes
Cook time: 10 minutes

Salsa, or "sauce" in Spanish, is the most popular condiment consumed in North America. The red variety is probably the one people are most familiar with, but green salsa is a great change of pace. Also known as salsa verde, this salsa is raw or cooked tomatillos and jalapeño peppers. When using fresh salsa, be sure to pay attention to the heat level.

1 CUP PREPARED GREEN CHILI SALSA
4 EGGS, AT ROOM TEMPERATURE
¼ CUP GRATED SHARP CHEDDAR CHEESE
SEA SALT AND FRESHLY GROUND PEPPER
TWO 6-INCH FLOUR TORTILLAS

1. In a large skillet coated with cooking spray over medium heat, heat the salsa verde.

2. Cook, stirring occasionally, until it bubbles, for about 3 minutes. Crack the eggs into the hot salsa and sprinkle the cheese over the eggs.

3. Cover and cook for about 4 minutes, or until the egg whites are cooked through.

4. Remove the skillet from the heat and season the eggs with salt and pepper.

5. Spoon the eggs, salsa, and cheese into the flour tortillas and roll them up.

6. Serve immediately.

Cauliflower Egg Curry

MAKES 4 SERVINGS

Prep time: 10 minutes
Cook time: 40 minutes

This is a simple but rich-tasting curry that is thickened from the added cauliflower. Cauliflower is a great source of vitamin A, fiber, vitamin K, folate, and potassium. It can help detox the body and lower the risk of cancer, heart disease, and inflammatory diseases such as Crohn's and irritable bowel syndrome.

2 TABLESPOONS OLIVE OIL
1 LARGE SWEET ONION, FINELY DICED
2 TEASPOONS MINCED GARLIC
1 TEASPOON GRATED FRESH GINGER
2 LARGE POTATOES, PEELED AND CUT INTO BITE-SIZE CHUNKS
3 TABLESPOONS CURRY PASTE
1 MEDIUM HEAD OF CAULIFLOWER, CUT INTO SMALL FLORETS
2 CUPS CANNED COCONUT MILK
8 HARD-BOILED EGGS (PAGE 35), PEELED AND HALVED LENGTHWISE
HOT COOKED BASMATI RICE
¼ CUP CHOPPED FRESH CILANTRO
¼ CUP CHOPPED CASHEWS

1. In a large deep skillet over medium heat, heat the oil.

2. Add the onion, garlic, and ginger and sauté until softened, about 5 minutes.

3. Add the potatoes and cook for 5 more minutes, stirring frequently.

4. Stir in the curry paste and cauliflower, and stir to coat.

5. Add the coconut milk and stir to combine.

6. Bring the mixture to a boil. Reduce the heat to low, and simmer, partially covered, for about 20 minutes, or until the sauce is slightly thickened and the vegetables are tender.

7. Add the eggs and simmer for 1 to 2 minutes until they are heated through.

8. Spoon the mixture over servings of the basmati rice, and top with cilantro and cashews.

Ratatouille with Poached Eggs

MAKES 4 SERVINGS

Prep time: 15 minutes
Cook time: 45 minutes

The flavorful stew accompanying these perfectly poached eggs is the epitome of comfort food. Ratatouille hails from France and is thought to have been created as a way to use up abundant summertime vegetables. The success of this dish is dependent on the freshness of your vegetables, and it is important not to throw them all together all at once during the cooking process. Each vegetable has a different cooking time.

1 TABLESPOON OLIVE OIL
1 LARGE SWEET ONION, CHOPPED
1 RED BELL PEPPER, SEEDED AND THINLY SLICED
2 TEASPOONS MINCED GARLIC
1 SMALL EGGPLANT, DICED
2 ZUCCHINI, DICED
ONE 14.5-OUNCE CAN DICED TOMATOES, UNDRAINED
½ CUP VEGETABLE BROTH OR WATER
1 TABLESPOON BALSAMIC VINEGAR
1 TABLESPOON CHOPPED FRESH OREGANO
PINCH OF RED PEPPER FLAKES
4 EGGS

1. In a large skillet over medium-high heat, heat the oil.

2. Add the onion, pepper, and garlic and sauté until the vegetables are softened, about 3 minutes.

3. Add the eggplant and the zucchini and for sauté 3 more minutes.

4. Add the tomatoes, vegetable broth, and vinegar.

5. Bring the mixture to a boil. Reduce the heat to low and simmer, uncovered, for 30 minutes.

6. Stir in the oregano and the red pepper flakes.

7. Make 4 deep wells in the tomato mixture and crack 1 egg into each hole.

8. Cover and cook 3 to 4 more minutes, or until the egg whites are firm.

Veggie Scrambled Eggs

MAKES 2 SERVINGS

Prep time: 5 minutes
Cook time: 10 minutes

While this dish won't win the beauty pageant, the taste more than makes up for its humble appearance. The goat cheese plays an important role in the excellent flavor. Goat cheese imparts a tangy taste and lovely creaminess to the eggs. This soft cheese is actually quite healthy as well as delicious. It is high in protein while being low in fat and calories. Goat cheese is also a wonderful choice for those who are lactose intolerant because it does not produce the same issues as cow milk.

2 TABLESPOONS OLIVE OIL
½ CUP SLICED BUTTON OR CREMINI MUSHROOMS
½ SMALL SWEET ONION, CHOPPED
½ GREEN BELL PEPPER, SEEDED AND CHOPPED
½ RED BELL PEPPER, SEEDED AND CHOPPED
1 SMALL TOMATO, CHOPPED
4 EGGS
¼ CUP 2 PERCENT MILK
¼ CUP GOAT CHEESE
FRESHLY GROUND PEPPER

1. In a large skillet over medium-high heat, heat the oil.

2. Add the mushrooms, onion, and peppers and sauté until the vegetables are softened, about 4 minutes.

3. In a small bowl, whisk together the tomato, eggs, and milk.

4. Add the egg mixture to the skillet and scramble until the eggs form large, cooked curds.

5. Stir in the goat cheese and season with pepper.

6. Serve warm.

Rolled Omelet with Spinach

MAKES 4 SERVINGS

Prep time: 15 minutes
Cook time: 30 minutes

This is a savory timesaving jelly-roll-style omelet that eliminates the need to stand over a stove to make individual omelets. It is perfect when you need to feed a bunch of people quickly. You can certainly add other ingredients to this dish, such as chopped herbs and meat, if you'd like. It is important to cut your filling ingredients finely and avoid over-stuffing so that the omelet rolls easily.

OLIVE OIL COOKING SPRAY
1 CUP 2 PERCENT MILK
½ CUP ALL-PURPOSE FLOUR
8 EGGS
1 TABLESPOON DIJON MUSTARD
SEA SALT AND FRESHLY GROUND PEPPER
3 CUPS THINLY SLICED SPINACH
1 LARGE TOMATO, DICED
1½ CUPS GRATED SWISS CHEESE

1. Preheat oven to 350°F.

2. Coat a rimmed 10-by-15-inch jelly-roll pan with cooking spray. Line the pan with parchment paper or aluminum foil and coat with additional cooking spray. Set aside.

3. In a large bowl, whisk together the milk and flour. Whisk in the eggs and mustard.

4. Pour the mixture evenly into the prepared pan.

5. Sprinkle the spinach evenly over the egg mixture and sprinkle the tomatoes over the spinach.

6. Bake the omelet until the sides are set, about 10 minutes.

7. Remove the omelet from the oven and sprinkle with the cheese.

8. Return the omelet to the oven and bake until the cheese is melted, about 4 minutes.

9. Lift the short-sided edge of the parchment paper and roll the omelet up tightly, peeling the parchment away as you roll.

10. Cut the omelet into slices before serving.

Eggs in Bell Peppers

MAKES 2 SERVINGS

Prep time: 5 minutes
Cook time: 10 minutes

Anyone who has ever used an egg ring to make perfect symmetrical sunny-side up eggs in a commercial kitchen will appreciate the ingenious vegetable ring in this recipe. You can use any color bell pepper for this dish, but it is important to find peppers with firm skin and flesh along with a diameter that will provide enough room for your eggs to spread out well.

1 TABLESPOON OLIVE OIL
1 LARGE RED BELL PEPPER, SEEDED AND CUT INTO FOUR ½-INCH-THICK RINGS
4 EGGS
SEA SALT AND FRESHLY GROUND PEPPER
2 TABLESPOONS GRATED PARMESAN CHEESE
4 THICK SLICES BREAD, TOASTED

1. In a large skillet over medium-high heat, heat the oil.

2. Arrange the peppers in a single layer in the pan and cook for 1 minute. Turn the peppers over.

3. Crack 1 egg into each pepper ring and lightly season with salt and pepper.

4. Cook until the egg whites are set but the egg yolks are still runny, about 3 minutes.

5. Sprinkle the eggs with the Parmesan cheese and place each on a slice of toast.

Easy Egg Curry

MAKES 4 SERVINGS

Prep time: 15 minutes
Cook time: 15 minutes

There are countless kinds of curry that vary in heat and color. This simple egg curry is north Indian, with garlic, tomatoes, and a complex layering of spices of an Asian flare. Southern Indian curries often feature coconut milk and are much spicier than the northern-style cuisine.

Chef's Tip: *If tomatoes are out of season, you can use a can of diced tomatoes instead of fresh. Just be sure to add 1 teaspoon of sugar to offset the acidity of the canned product.*

2 TABLESPOONS OLIVE OIL

1 LARGE ONION, CHOPPED

2 LARGE TOMATOES, DICED

2 FRESH GREEN CHILES, MINCED

2 TEASPOONS MINCED GARLIC

2 TEASPOONS GRATED FRESH GINGER

1 CUP UNSWEETENED CANNED COCONUT MILK

1 TABLESPOON GROUND CORIANDER

1 TEASPOON GROUND CUMIN

½ TEASPOON TURMERIC

½ TEASPOON CHILI POWDER

8 HARD-BOILED EGGS (PAGE 35), QUARTERED

SEA SALT

HOT COOKED BASMATI RICE

1 TABLESPOON CHOPPED FRESH CILANTRO

1. In a large skillet over medium-high heat, heat the oil.

2. Add the onion and sauté until it is softened and lightly caramelized, about 7 minutes.

3. Add the tomato, chiles, garlic, and ginger and sauté for 2 more minutes.

4. Add the coconut milk, coriander, cumin, turmeric, and chili powder and bring the sauce to a simmer.

5. Add the eggs and season with salt.

6. Continue simmering until the eggs are heated through, about 5 minutes.

7. Spoon servings over basmati rice and sprinkle with cilantro.

Eggs Baked in Tomatoes

MAKES 2 SERVINGS

Prep time: 10 minutes
Cook time: 15 minutes

This dish is messy to eat but worth every bite. The tomatoes soften, and when you cut into them, the whole dish falls apart in a delicious heap. You will want to scoop up every drop of liquid with toast or bread because the flavors are absolutely divine.

4 MEDIUM TOMATOES
1 TEASPOON OLIVE OIL
4 EGGS
2 TABLESPOONS CHOPPED FRESH PARSLEY
PINCH OF SEA SALT
PINCH OF FRESHLY GROUND PEPPER
¼ CUP GRATED ASIAGO CHEESE

1. Preheat the broiler to high.

2. Cut the top off the stem end of the tomatoes. Carefully scoop out the pulp and seeds from the tomatoes. Reserve the scooped out portion for another use.

3. Carefully scoop out the pulp and seeds from the tomatoes. Reserve the scooped out portion for another use.

4. Place the tomatoes, cut-sides-down, on paper towels for 10 minutes to drain.

5. In a baking dish, place the tomatoes cut-sides-up. Drizzle the tomatoes with olive oil.

6. In a small bowl, whisk together the eggs, parsley, salt, and pepper until blended.

7. Spoon the egg mixture evenly into the tomatoes.

8. Sprinkle with cheese.

9. Broil the tomatoes until the egg is cooked through, about 5 minutes.

Asparagus and Goat Cheese Quiche

MAKES 6 SERVINGS

Prep time: 15 minutes
Cook time: 25 minutes

Elegant with chunks of creamy goat cheese and vibrant asparagus, this quiche is perfect for a wedding shower or light brunch on a sunny patio. For a lighter meal, cut the quiche into eight servings since it is so rich.

5 EGGS

1½ CUPS WHIPPING CREAM

¼ CUP CHOPPED FRESH CHIVES

PINCH OF SEA SALT

PINCH OF FRESHLY GROUND PEPPER

ONE 9-INCH DEEP-DISH PIE CRUST

1 CUP COOKED ASPARAGUS, COARSELY CHOPPED

1 CUP CRUMBLED GOAT CHEESE

½ CUP GRATED WHITE CHEDDAR CHEESE

1. Preheat the oven to 350°F.

2. In a medium bowl, whisk together the eggs, whipping cream, chives, salt, and pepper until thoroughly blended.

3. In the pie crust, spread the asparagus and the crumbled goat cheese evenly. Pour the egg mixture over the asparagus.

4. Sprinkle the quiche evenly with Cheddar cheese.

5. Bake the quiche for 25 to 30 minutes. Serve warm.

Arugula and Fennel Omelets

MAKES 2 SERVINGS

Prep time: 5 minutes
Cook time: 15 minutes

Your taste buds will wake up and take notice of the interesting contrasts of flavors in this dish. The licorice flavor of the fennel pairs well with the mild eggs and peppery snap of arugula.

Timesaving Tip: *When you use a fennel bulb for recipes, don't discard the fronds. Chop and store them in a zip-top plastic bag in the freezer for future use. The frozen fronds will not be as crisp as fresh, but the taste will remain and you can add them to a dish like this omelet with great results.*

1 TABLESPOON BUTTER

4 EGGS

¼ CUP WHOLE MILK

1 TABLESPOON CHOPPED FRESH CHERVIL OR BASIL

1 TABLESPOON CHOPPED FRESH CHIVES

1 TABLESPOON CHOPPED FENNEL FRONDS

½ CUP CHOPPED ARUGULA

½ CUP GRATED SHARP CHEDDAR CHEESE

SEA SALT AND FRESHLY GROUND PEPPER

1. In a small nonstick skillet or omelet pan over medium-high heat, melt half of the butter.

2. In a small bowl, whisk together the eggs, milk, chervil, chives, fennel, and arugula.

3. Pour half of the egg mixture into the pan and gently swirl the pan.

4. As the egg mixture cooks, lift the edges to allow the uncooked egg to flow underneath.

5. When the egg is set, sprinkle half of the Cheddar cheese on top, and season with salt and pepper.

6. Flip the omelet in half and slide onto a serving plate.

7. Repeat the process with the remaining butter, egg mixture, and cheese.

8. Serve immediately.

Individual Chile Casseroles

MAKES 4 SERVINGS

Prep time: 10 minutes
Cook time: 30 minutes

You can certainly make these individual servings as one larger casserole if you don't have ramekins. Simply combine the ingredients according the recipe directions, bake in an 8-inch baking dish, and increase the baking time by about 10 minutes. Scoop out onto plates with a nice salad for a great lunch or dinner.

TWO 4-OUNCE CANS DICED GREEN CHILES, DRAINED AND PATTED DRY

1 CUP FRESH OR CANNED CORN KERNELS

2 GREEN ONIONS, SLICED

1 CUP GRATED MONTEREY JACK CHEESE

6 EGG WHITES

4 EGGS

1½ CUPS 2 PERCENT MILK

SEA SALT AND FRESHLY GROUND PEPPER

1. Preheat the oven to 400°F.

2. Coat four 10-ounce ramekins with cooking spray and place them on a rimmed baking sheet; set aside.

3. Divide the green chiles, corn, and green onion evenly among the ramekins. Top each evenly with Monterey Jack cheese.

4. In a medium bowl, whisk together the egg whites, eggs, milk, salt, and pepper until thoroughly combined.

5. Divide the egg mixture evenly among the ramekins.

6. Bake the casseroles until the eggs are set and the tops are browned, about 30 minutes.

7. Serve warm.

Tasty Spinach Cakes

MAKES 4 SERVINGS

Prep time: 15 minutes
Total time: 40 minutes

These nutrient-packed muffin-style omelets can also be made in paper muffin liners, but the edges will not be as browned. Don't be intimidated by the amount of spinach used in this recipe. It shrinks after it cooks.

Chef's Tip: *Try to buy spinach that is stored in direct light whenever possible because it actually has more nutrients than greens stored in the dark. Cooking the spinach also increases the available nutrients by as much as three times over raw spinach.*

12 OUNCES FRESH SPINACH, FINELY CHOPPED
3 EGGS
½ CUP COTTAGE CHEESE
½ CUP GRATED PARMESAN CHEESE
1 TEASPOON MINCED GARLIC
PINCH OF SEA SALT
PINCH OF FRESHLY GROUND PEPPER
2 TABLESPOONS CHOPPED FRESH DILL

1. Preheat the oven to 400°F.

2. Coat 8 cups in a muffin pan with cooking spray; set aside.

3. In a medium bowl, stir together the spinach, eggs, cottage cheese, Parmesan cheese, garlic, salt, and pepper.

4. Divide the mixture evenly among the prepared muffin cups.

5. Bake the spinach cakes until the eggs are set, about 20 minutes.

6. Let the spinach cakes stand in the muffin pan for 5 minutes.

7. Gently run a knife around the edges of the cups and turn the cakes out onto a serving plate. Sprinkle each serving with dill.

Egg Stir-Fry

MAKES 4 SERVINGS

Prep time: 15 minutes
Cook time: 15 minutes

This recipe uses a thin omelet sliced into strips as noodles. Try not to stir the ingredients vigorously at the end of the cooking process or you risk breaking the longer pieces of omelet.

8 LARGE EGGS

¼ CUP WATER

2 TABLESPOONS ALL-PURPOSE FLOUR

PINCH OF SEA SALT

1 TEASPOON OLIVE OIL OR CANOLA OIL

1 TEASPOON MINCED GARLIC

1 TEASPOON GRATED FRESH GINGER

2 TABLESPOONS SOY SAUCE

3 MEDIUM CARROTS, PEELED AND SLICED

1 CUP SNOW PEAS, TRIMMED

1 LARGE RED BELL PEPPER, SEEDED AND CUT INTO STRIPS

1 LARGE YELLOW PEPPER, SEEDED AND CUT INTO STRIPS

1 CUP BEAN SPROUTS

3 GREEN ONIONS, DIAGONALLY SLICED

HOT COOKED RICE

1 TABLESPOON SESAME SEEDS

1. In a small bowl, whisk together the eggs, water, flour, and salt; set aside.

2. In a large skillet over medium-high heat, heat the oil. Add the garlic, ginger, and soy sauce and sauté for about 1 minute.

3. Add the carrots, snow peas, peppers, and bean sprouts.

4. Stir-fry until the vegetables are crisp-tender, about 5 minutes.

5. Remove the vegetables from the skillet with a slotted spoon and set aside.

continued ▶

6. Return the skillet to medium-high heat.

7. Add the green onions and egg mixture; stir to combine.

8. As the egg mixture sets around the edges, lift the cooked portion and allow the uncooked egg to flow under to the skillet.

9. Cook until the eggs are set, about 5 minutes.

10. Transfer the omelet to a cutting board and cut into long strips.

11. Return the vegetable mixture to the skillet and gently stir in the egg strips.

12. Spoon the stir-fry evenly over servings of rice. Sprinkle each serving with sesame seeds.

CHAPTER TWELVE

Paleo Entrées

Chicken Frittata with Mushrooms and Kale

MAKES 4 SERVINGS

Prep time: 15 minutes
Cook time: 35 minutes

Kale is often referred to as a super food because of its vast array of nutrients and antioxidant power. Kale is very high in iron, vitamin A, vitamin K, fiber, and calcium. It can help reduce the risk of cancer, cardiovascular disease, and help detox the body. Kale can also boost your metabolism, so this frittata is a wonderful way to start the day.

. . . .

Timesaving Tip: *If you are following a Paleo diet, save some prep time by cooking a large quantity of chicken breasts to use in your recipes all week. Simply store them in the refrigerator in sealed plastic zip-top bags and take one (or two) out when you need them.*

. . . .

1 TEASPOON OLIVE OIL

1 CUP SLICED BUTTON OR CREMINI MUSHROOMS

½ SMALL SWEET ONION, CHOPPED

1 TEASPOON MINCED GARLIC

2 CUPS KALE, CHOPPED

2 SMALL ZUCCHINI, CUT INTO THIN STRIPS

TWO 6-OUNCE BONELESS SKINLESS CHICKEN BREASTS, COOKED AND DICED

6 EGGS, BEATEN

FRESHLY GROUND PEPPER

¼ CUP PREPARED BASIL PESTO

1. Preheat the oven to 375°F.

2. In a large skillet over medium-high heat, heat the oil.

3. Add the mushrooms, onion, and garlic and sauté until the vegetables are softened, about 3 minutes.

4. Add the kale and zucchini and cook until the kale is wilted, about 2 minutes.

5. Add the cooked chicken and stir to combine.

6. Pour the eggs into the skillet and cook for 2 more minutes, without stirring, until the egg is set on the bottom.

7. Bake the frittata for about 20 minutes or until a knife inserted in the center comes out clean.

8. Season each serving with pepper and 1 tablespoon of basil pesto.

Root Vegetable Bacon Hash

MAKES 4 SERVINGS

Prep time: 15 minutes
Cook time: 15 minutes

Some Paleo enthusiasts stay away from root vegetables because they think they are too starchy for this eating plan. Although these vegetables do fall on the starchier end of the spectrum, they are also packed with nutrients and fiber, which is crucial when consuming a lot of protein. Shredding the vegetables helps them cook faster, and for a crispier hash, sauté the vegetables a little longer in additional oil.

6 SLICES BACON, CHOPPED
½ POUND LEAN TURKEY SAUSAGE
1 TEASPOON MINCED GARLIC
1 SMALL SWEET POTATO, PEELED AND SHREDDED
½ CELERY ROOT, PEELED AND SHREDDED
1 CARROT, PEELED AND SHREDDED
2 PARSNIPS, PEELED AND SHREDDED
½ SMALL SWEET ONION, THINLY SLICED
6 EGGS
SEA SALT AND FRESHLY GROUND PEPPER

1. In a large skillet over medium-high heat, cook the bacon and sausage until browned, about 6 minutes. Remove the bacon mixture from the skillet to a bowl with a slotted spoon. Reserve 2 tablespoons drippings in the skillet.

2. Add the garlic, the shredded vegetables, and the onion to the skillet and sauté until the vegetables are browned and tender, about 7 minutes.

3. Return the bacon and sausage to the skillet.

4. Add the eggs and cook until the eggs are completely cooked.

5. Season with salt and pepper and serve immediately.

Stuffed Acorn Squash

MAKES 4 SERVINGS

Prep time: 20 minutes
Cook time: 15 minutes

Acorn squash is a wonderful cold-weather vegetable often overlooked for its cousin, butternut squash. Because it can be hard to cut, try piercing the squash a few times with the tines of a fork and microwave on high 1 to 2 minutes. Acorn squash is worth the effort because it is a great source of vitamin C, vitamin A, vitamin B_6, and folate.

. . . .

Timesaving Tip: *This entire dish can be prepared ahead of time and simply baked when you want to serve the meal. You can also cook the squash in advance and refrigerate it in a sealed container along with the covered squash shells. Warm up the scooped out squash in the skillet along with the other ingredients before stuffing the shells.*

. . . .

2 ACORN SQUASH, HALVED AND SEEDED

1 POUND LEAN GROUND BEEF

1 SMALL SWEET ONION, DICED

1 GREEN BELL PEPPER, DICED

1 TEASPOON MINCED GARLIC

4 EGGS

SEA SALT AND FRESHLY GROUND PEPPER

1. Preheat the oven to 400°F.

2. In a large baking sheet, arrange the acorn squash, cut-sides-down.

3. Bake the squash until soft, about 20 minutes.

4. Remove the squash from the oven and let it cool, about 15 minutes.

5. Meanwhile, in a large skillet over medium-high heat, add the lean ground beef.

continued ▶

Stuffed Acorn Squash *continued* ▶

6. Cook the beef until it is no longer pink, about 5 minutes.

7. Add the onion, bell pepper, and garlic to the skillet and sauté until the vegetables are softened, about 4 minutes.

8. Scoop out most of the squash flesh from the skin and add it to the beef mixture, mixing well.

9. Spoon the filling evenly into the squash shells.

10. Make a small well in the top of the filling of each squash. Place 1 egg into each well.

11. Bake the squash for 10 minutes or until the egg whites are firm and the egg yolks are still runny.

Classic Steak and Eggs

MAKES 2 SERVINGS

Prep time: 5 minutes
Cook time: 14 minutes

What Paleo meal plan would be complete without the addition of classic steak and eggs? This dish practically screams Paleo! You can use one skillet to prepare all the components of the meal if you would rather not use two. Make the onions first and keep them warm, followed by the steak so that it can rest, and finish with the eggs. You don't even really have to wipe the skillet in between the components!

2 TABLESPOONS OLIVE OIL
TWO 6-OUNCE NEW YORK STRIP STEAKS
SEA SALT AND FRESHLY GROUND PEPPER
1 SMALL SWEET ONION, THINLY SLICED
4 EGGS

1. In 2 large skillets over medium-high heat, heat 1 tablespoon of olive oil in each.

2. Season the steaks on both sides with salt and pepper.

3. Add the onion to one skillet and the steaks to the other skillet.

4. Sauté the onions until they caramelize, about 6 minutes.

5. Cook the steaks 4 minutes on both sides or to desired doneness.

6. Remove the steaks from the skillet and top with the onions.

7. Return one skillet to medium-high heat. Add the eggs and cook 4 minutes or to desired doneness. Serve eggs with steaks.

Paleo Breakfast Stew

MAKES 3 SERVINGS

Prep time: 5 minutes
Cook time: 15 minutes

Substitute any type of meat for the sausage in this dish and still love the tasty results. If you use chicken breast, then add 1 teaspoon of oil before cooking the meat or it will stick. The rendered fat from the sausage will be missing, so you need to replace it.

½ POUND SPICY CHICKEN SAUSAGE

1 SMALL SWEET ONION, THINLY SLICED

1 TEASPOON MINCED GARLIC

3 LARGE TOMATOES, DICED

2 TABLESPOONS TOMATO PASTE

½ CUP LOW-SODIUM CHICKEN BROTH

1 CUP DICED HAM

1 TEASPOON CHILI POWDER

1 CUP SPINACH

DASH OF SEA SALT

DASH OF FRESHLY GROUND PEPPER

2 TEASPOONS WHITE VINEGAR

3 EGGS

1. In a large skillet over medium-high heat, add the sausage and sauté until completely cooked, about 5 minutes.

2. Add the onions and garlic and sauté until translucent, about 4 minutes.

3. Add the tomatoes, tomato paste, chicken broth, ham, and chili powder; stir to combine.

4. Add the spinach and season with salt and pepper.

5. Simmer until the flavors are blended, about 5 minutes.

6. While the stew is simmering, in a medium saucepan over medium heat, bring 3 to 4 inches of water and the vinegar to a simmer.

7. Crack 1 egg into a small bowl and pour it into the water.

8. Repeat the process with the remaining eggs.

9. Cook the eggs until the egg whites are firm, about 3 minutes.

10. Remove the eggs with a slotted spoon and place them on paper towels to drain.

11. Divide the stew evenly among serving plates and top each serving with 1 poached egg.

Omelet Muffins

MAKES 8 MUFFINS

Prep time: 10 minutes
Cook time: 15 minutes

These "muffins" are basically individual frittatas that cook up in a snap. You can make these handheld omelets and freeze them for a convenient snack or quick breakfast during a busy week. Just store them wrapped in zip-top plastic bags and take them out the night before to thaw in the refrigerator overnight, or microwave them straight from the freezer.

COOKING SPRAY
8 EGGS
8 OUNCES COOKED HAM, FINELY DICED
1 SMALL RED BELL PEPPER, SEEDED AND FINELY DICED
1 SMALL SWEET ONION, FINELY DICED
PINCH OF SEA SALT
PINCH OF FRESHLY GROUND PEPPER
2 TABLESPOONS WATER

1. Preheat the oven to 350°F.

2. Coat 8 muffin cups with cooking spray; set aside.

3. In a large bowl, whisk together all of the remaining ingredients until thoroughly combined.

4. Divide the egg mixture evenly among the muffin cups.

5. Bake the muffins until the eggs are set and puffed, about 15 minutes.

6. Remove the muffins from the oven and let stand for 5 minutes.

7. Gently run a knife around the edges of the muffins and turn them out onto a serving plate.

8. Serve warm or cold.

Chicken Egg Casserole

MAKES 4 SERVINGS

Prep time: 15 minutes
Cook time: 45 minutes

The butter in this recipe is made from milk from cows who have grazed on grass rather than commercial feed. Why is this important? Grass-fed cows usually produce milk that is more nutritious and not filled with unhealthy hormones or antibiotics. Many Paleo enthusiasts go one step further and find unpasteurized milk right from the farmer to avoid ingredients added during the commercial production of milk. Butter is sometimes a gray area in this diet, but it is a healthy fat, and grass-fed cows simply make the product more attractive for those following a healthy lifestyle.

½ CUP GRASS-FED BUTTER, MELTED

2 LEEKS, CLEANED AND CHOPPED

6 EGGS

1 CUP CANNED COCONUT MILK

THREE 8-OUNCE BONELESS, SKINLESS CHICKEN BREASTS, COOKED AND SHREDDED

1½ TEASPOONS CURRY POWDER

½ TEASPOON GROUND CUMIN

PINCH OF GROUND CORIANDER

SEA SALT AND FRESHLY GROUND PEPPER

1. Preheat the oven to 400°F.

2. Use 2 tablespoons melted butter to grease a 2-quart dish; set aside.

3. In a large skillet over medium heat, heat 2 tablespoons melted butter.

4. Add the leeks and sauté until they are soft, about 3 minutes. Remove the skillet from the heat and set aside.

5. In a large bowl, whisk together the eggs, remaining melted butter, and coconut milk until frothy, about 2 minutes.

6. Add the leeks, shredded chicken, curry powder, cumin, and coriander to the egg mixture and mix well.

continued ▶

7. Season with salt and pepper.

8. Pour the egg mixture into the prepared dish.

9. Bake the casserole until puffy and lightly browned, about 35 minutes.

10. Serve warm.

Individual Turkey Tomato Casseroles

MAKES 4 SERVINGS

Prep time: 10 minutes
Cook time: 10 minutes

This is a wonderful way to use up leftover turkey from Thanksgiving and is a great alternative to soup! Turkey is a great choice for a Paleo diet too, especially organic pasture-raised turkey, because it is high in protein and contains all the B vitamins as well as omega-3 fatty acids. This is important for stabilized blood sugar and a decreased risk of cancer.

. . . .

Timesaving Tip: *This dish is already quick to prepare, but it can be made even quicker by assembling the casseroles and storing them in the refrigerator up to the day before baking them. You can also roast a turkey breast at the beginning of the week and portion it in the fridge for quick recipes like this one.*

. . . .

COOKING SPRAY
12 OUNCES COOKED TURKEY BREAST, SHREDDED
16 GRAPE TOMATOES, HALVED
2 TABLESPOONS CHOPPED FRESH BASIL
8 EGGS
SEA SALT AND FRESHLY GROUND PEPPER
2 TABLESPOONS HEAVY CREAM

1. Preheat the oven to 350°F.

2. Coat four 8-ounce ramekins with cooking spray; set aside.

3. Divide the turkey, tomatoes, and basil evenly among the ramekins.

4. Crack 2 eggs into each ramekin and season with salt and pepper.

5. Spoon 1½ teaspoons of the cream over each ramekin.

6. Place ramekins on a baking sheet and bake for about 10 minutes, or until the egg whites are cooked through.

7. Heat the broiler to high and broil the eggs for 1 minute.

8. Serve immediately.

Easy Ham Burritos

MAKES 2 SERVINGS

Prep time: 5 minutes
Cook time: 15 minutes

These burritos use thin ham slices in place of tortillas. The trick to creating burritos that stay rolled up is not to use ham slices that are too thick or too cold. Try rolling your ham slices without filling to see if they spring back before using the slices as tortilla stand-ins.

1 TEASPOON OLIVE OIL
¼ SMALL SWEET ONION, DICED
½ RED BELL PEPPER, SEEDED AND DICED
1 SMALL TOMATO, DICED
½ CUP THINLY SLICED SPINACH
4 EGGS, BEATEN
SEA SALT AND FRESHLY GROUND PEPPER
4 LARGE, THIN SLICES OF HAM

1. In a medium skillet over medium heat, heat the oil.

2. Add the onion and pepper and sauté until softened, about 3 minutes.

3. Add the tomato and spinach and sauté 1 more minute.

4. Add the eggs and scramble until large, cooked curds are formed and there is no visible liquid.

5. Season with salt and pepper.

6. Arrange the ham slices on a clean cutting board and spoon the eggs evenly into the middle of each piece.

7. Roll up the ham like a burrito and return to the skillet over medium heat.

8. Cook the burritos until the ham is hot, about 3 minutes.

9. Serve immediately.

Layered Omelet Cake

MAKES 8 SERVINGS

Prep time: 25 minutes
Cook time: 35 minutes

This dish is inspired by stacked egg foo young omelets and uses a spring-form pan to contain the omelets in a neat unfolded stack. This recipe includes raw-milk cheese, which can be found at organic grocery stores and health food markets.

10 EGGS
¼ CUP WATER
½ TEASPOON HOT PEPPER SAUCE
OLIVE OIL COOKING SPRAY
1 TEASPOON OLIVE OIL
1 SWEET ONION, DICED
2 TEASPOONS MINCED GARLIC
2 CUPS SPINACH
1½ CUPS GRATED GRASS-FED RAW CHEESE, DIVIDED
2 TABLESPOONS CHOPPED FRESH CHIVES
SEA SALT AND FRESHLY GROUND PEPPER

1. Preheat the oven to 375°F.

2. In a medium bowl, whisk together the eggs, water, and hot sauce until thoroughly blended.

3. In an 8-inch nonstick skillet coated with cooking spray over medium heat, add ½ cup of the egg mixture.

4. As the egg mixture cooks, lift the edges to allow the uncooked egg to flow underneath. Cook 2 minutes, or until done, and slide the omelet onto a plate.

5. Repeat the same process with the remaining egg mixture to make 5 omelets; set aside.

6. Return the skillet to medium heat and heat the olive oil.

7. Add the onion and garlic and sauté until softened, about 3 minutes.

continued ▶

8. Add the spinach and cook until wilted, about 2 minutes.

9. Coat a 9-inch spring-form pan with cooking spray.

10. Place 1 omelet in the bottom of the pan. Top with one-quarter of the vegetables and cheese.

11. Repeat layers with the remaining omelets, vegetables, and cheese.

12. Place the spring-form pan on baking sheet and bake until browned and heated through, about 30 minutes.

13. Let the omelet cake stand for 10 minutes before serving.

CHAPTER THIRTEEN

Lunch and Dinner Entrées

Italian Fennel Pie

MAKES 6 SERVINGS

Prep time: 15 minutes
Cook time: 50 minutes

Not in the mood to make pie crust from scratch? Then this is the perfect quiche for you! It uses bread crumbs as the crust to contain the tasty filling. It is also studded with sautéed slices of fennel, which complements the anise-flavored Italian sausage taste beautifully. Look for sausage that has fennel seeds in the ingredient list to get this doubling of flavor.

2 TABLESPOONS BUTTER
¼ CUP DRY BREAD CRUMBS
½ CUP GRATED MOZZARELLA CHEESE
1 SMALL SWEET ONION, CHOPPED
½ FENNEL BULB, THINLY SLICED
1 TEASPOON MINCED GARLIC
6 OUNCES ITALIAN CHICKEN SAUSAGE LINKS, COOKED AND SLICED
SEA SALT AND FRESHLY GROUND PEPPER
3 EGGS
1 CUP HALF-AND-HALF

1. Preheat the oven to 350°F.

2. Use about 1 teaspoon of butter to grease a 10-inch pie plate.

3. Sprinkle the bread crumbs evenly over the butter in the pie plate.

4. Sprinkle the cheese evenly over the bread crumbs and set the pie plate aside.

5. In a large skillet over medium heat, melt the remaining butter.

6. Add the onion, fennel, and garlic to the skillet and sauté until the vegetables are softened, about 5 minutes.

7. Stir in the sausage and sauté about 1 to 2 minutes. Season with salt and pepper and remove from the heat.

8. In a small bowl, whisk together the eggs and the half-and-half.

9. Spoon the vegetable mixture evenly into the pie plate and pour the egg mixture over the vegetables.

10. Bake the pie for about 30 minutes, or until set.

11. Let stand 5 minutes before serving.

Tortilla Egg Casserole

MAKES 4 SERVINGS

Prep time: 15 minutes
Cook time: 30 minutes

This one-pot meal is sure to become a family favorite with its cheesy and spicy ingredients and tortillas to soak up the custard for the perfect texture. Since it is made in advance, dinner is a snap. Don't skip the step of refrigerating the casserole overnight or at least for 6 hours; the tortillas need time to absorb the liquid.

Chef's Tip: *This recipe can be adapted to create endless variations as long as the custard base and tortilla layers remain constant. You can layer mushrooms, thinly sliced greens, and even frozen vegetables for a change.*

COOKING SPRAY

SIX 8-INCH FLOUR TORTILLAS, HALVED

TWO 4.5-OUNCE CANS CHOPPED GREEN CHILES, DRAINED AND RINSED

1 LARGE RED BELL PEPPER, SEEDED AND FINELY CHOPPED

4 CUPS GRATED SHARP CHEDDAR OR MONTEREY JACK CHEESE

5 EGGS, BEATEN

2 CUPS 2 PERCENT MILK

PINCH OF SEA SALT

PINCH OF FRESHLY GROUND PEPPER

1. Coat a 9-by-13-inch baking dish with cooking spray.

2. Place 4 tortilla halves in the bottom of the dish to cover the bottom as much as possible.

3. Sprinkle the tortillas evenly with half of the chiles, half of the red bell pepper, and one-third of the cheese.

4. Repeat the process with the remaining tortilla halves, chiles, pepper, and cheese.

5. In a small bowl, whisk together the eggs, milk, salt, and pepper. Pour the egg mixture over the layered tortilla mixture.

continued ▶

Tortilla Egg Casserole *continued* ▶

6. Cover the casserole and refrigerate overnight.

7. Preheat the oven to 350°F.

8. Bake the casserole for 30 minutes until it is set and browned.

9. Let the casserole stand 10 minutes before serving.

Brussels Sprouts Hash

MAKES 4 SERVINGS

Prep time: 10 minutes
Cook time: 20 minutes

Brussels sprouts often have a bad reputation, mainly because they have a cabbage-like odor, and people don't know how to prepare them. This recipe will make a Brussels sprouts fan out of even the hardest critic. Besides being tasty, they can also help reduce the risk of cancer, lower cholesterol, promote thyroid health, and stabilize blood sugar.

4 SLICES THICK-CUT BACON, CHOPPED
1 SMALL SWEET ONION, FINELY DICED
1 SWEET POTATO, PEELED AND CUT INTO ½-INCH CUBES
2 TEASPOONS MINCED GARLIC
12 BRUSSELS SPROUTS, TRIMMED AND SLICED
OLIVE OIL COOKING SPRAY
4 EGGS
SEA SALT AND FRESHLY GROUND PEPPER

1. In a large skillet over medium-high heat, cook the bacon until it is crispy.

2. Remove the bacon with a slotted spoon to paper towels to drain. Reserve the drippings in the skillet.

3. Reduce the heat to medium. Add the onion and sweet potato and sauté until the sweet potato is tender, about 5 minutes.

4. Add the garlic and sauté 1 more minute.

5. Add the Brussels sprouts to the skillet and stir to combine.

6. Sauté, stirring constantly, until the Brussels sprouts are tender and lightly browned, about 5 minutes. Remove the skillet from the heat and set aside.

7. In a small skillet coated with cooking spray over medium-high heat, cook the eggs until desired doneness.

8. Divide the hash evenly among serving plates and top each serving with 1 egg. Season with salt and pepper.

Spaghetti Carbonara

Prep time: 10 minutes

Cook time: 15 minutes

This is a lightened-up version of carbonara sauce, which traditionally features heavy cream, pancetta, and several types of cheese. If you'd like, the white wine can be replaced with chicken broth or vegetable broth plus 1 tablespoon white wine vinegar.

5 SLICES LEAN TURKEY BACON, CHOPPED

2 TEASPOONS MINCED GARLIC

½ CUP DRY WHITE WINE

ONE 12-OUNCE PACKAGE SPAGHETTI

5 EGGS

½ CUP EVAPORATED FAT-FREE MILK

¼ CUP CHOPPED FRESH PARSLEY

¼ CUP CHOPPED FRESH BASIL

½ CUP GRATED PARMESAN CHEESE

SEA SALT AND FRESHLY GROUND PEPPER

1. In a large skillet over medium-high heat, cook the bacon until it is crispy.

2. Add the garlic and sauté 1 more minute.

3. Whisk in the wine and bring the mixture to a boil.

4. Remove the skillet from the heat and let it stand for 10 minutes.

5. Cook the spaghetti according to package directions; drain.

6. In a small bowl, whisk together the eggs and the evaporated milk.

7. Add the egg mixture, parsley, and basil to the bacon mixture.

8. Return the skillet to medium-high heat and whisk constantly until the mixture thickens, about 5 minutes.

9. Stir in the Parmesan cheese and season with salt and pepper.

10. Remove the skillet from the heat and toss the sauce with the spaghetti.

11. Serve immediately.

Speedy Creamy Broccoli Pasta

MAKES 4 SERVINGS

Prep time: 5 minutes
Cook time: 15 minutes

The sauce created in this quick pasta dish is similar to alfredo sauce, but without the work. The cottage cheese and egg combine for an ultra-creamy result and the deep green broccoli is gorgeous. Use your favorite small pasta in this recipe if it's not elbow macaroni.

OLIVE OIL COOKING SPRAY
ONE 7-OUNCE PACKAGE ELBOW MACARONI, COOKED ACCORDING TO PACKAGE DIRECTIONS
2 CUPS COTTAGE CHEESE
3 CUPS CHOPPED COOKED BROCCOLI
4 EGGS
¼ CUP GRATED PARMESAN CHEESE
1 TABLESPOON CHOPPED FRESH PARSLEY
PINCH OF RED PEPPER FLAKES

1. In a large nonstick skillet coated with cooking spray over medium heat, add the pasta, cottage cheese, and broccoli, stirring well to combine.

2. Cook, stirring frequently, until the pasta is heated through, about 5 minutes.

3. Make 4 deep wells in the pasta with the back of a spoon.

4. Crack 1 egg into each well.

5. Cover and cook until the egg whites are completely set, about 5 minutes.

6. Divide mixture evenly among serving plates. Sprinkle each serving with the Parmesan cheese, the parsley, and the red pepper flakes.

Egg Foo Young

Prep time: 5 minutes
Cook time: 15 minutes

This egg foo young variation is more American than Asian, but the general ingredients and method are inspired from a traditional, more elaborate Chinese dish: Fu Yung Egg Slices. Add cooked chicken, shrimp, or even cooked pork to these tasty omelets if you want a more substantial meal.

1 TABLESPOON CANOLA OIL

1 TEASPOON GRATED FRESH GINGER

½ TEASPOON MINCED GARLIC

6 GREEN ONIONS, CHOPPED

1 STALK CELERY, CHOPPED

2 CUPS BEAN SPROUTS

½ CUP BUTTON OR CREMINI MUSHROOMS, SLICED

1 RED BELL PEPPER, SEEDED AND FINELY DICED

1 TEASPOON SEA SALT

6 EGGS, BEATEN

FRESHLY GROUND PEPPER

1. In a large skillet over medium-high heat, heat half of the oil.

2. Add the ginger and garlic and sauté for 1 minute.

3. Add the green onion, celery, bean sprouts, mushrooms, red bell pepper, and salt to the skillet and sauté until the vegetables are softened, about 5 minutes.

4. Transfer the vegetables to a large bowl and add the beaten egg.

5. Season with pepper and stir until thoroughly combined.

6. Wipe the skillet with a paper towel and add the remaining oil.

7. Return the skillet to medium high-heat and add about one-quarter of the egg mixture.

8. As the egg mixture cooks, lift the edges to allow the uncooked egg to flow underneath. Cook 2 minutes on each side, or until the eggs are browned and cooked through. Transfer to a plate.

9. Repeat the process with the remaining egg mixture.

10. Serve immediately.

Poached Egg Eggplant Stacks

MAKES 4 SERVINGS

Prep time: 15 minutes
Cook time: 15 minutes

If you have children (or adults) in the house who will not touch eggplant, you might change their minds with this flavorful stacked meal. They might not even notice the eggplant at the bottom because it's covered up with other delicious ingredients and a perfect runny yolk from the poached egg.

1 ITALIAN EGGPLANT, CUT CROSSWISE INTO FOUR ¼-INCH SLICES

OLIVE OIL FOR BRUSHING

SEA SALT

FOUR 2-OUNCE THIN SAUSAGE PATTIES

1 TEASPOON WHITE VINEGAR

4 EGGS

1 LARGE TOMATO, CUT INTO 4 SLICES

2 TABLESPOONS CHOPPED FRESH PARSLEY

2 TABLESPOONS GRATED PARMESAN CHEESE

FRESHLY GROUND PEPPER

1. Preheat the broiler to high.

2. Brush the eggplant on both sides with olive oil and sprinkle with salt.

3. Arrange the slices in one layer on a baking sheet and broil about 2 minutes on each side, or until they are tender.

4. Remove the baking sheet from the oven and set aside.

5. In a medium skillet over medium-high heat, cook the sausage patties completely, about 5 minutes. Remove from the heat and set aside.

6. In a medium saucepan over high heat, bring about 3 to 4 inches of water and the vinegar to a boil.

7. Reduce the heat to medium and maintain a gentle simmer.

continued ▶

8. Crack 1 egg into a small bowl.

9. Gently pour the egg into the simmering water and repeat the process with the remaining eggs.

10. Cook the eggs until the egg whites are firm, about 3 minutes.

11. Remove the poached eggs with a slotted spoon, and drain on a paper towel.

12. Place 1 eggplant slice on a serving plate and top with 1 tomato slice, 1 sausage patty, 1 poached egg, parsley, and Parmesan cheese.

13. Repeat the process with remaining ingredients to create 3 more stacks.

14. Season with pepper and serve.

Monte Cristo Egg Melt

MAKES 2 SERVINGS

Prep time: 10 minutes
Cook time: 5 minutes

This is the ultimate sandwich that is deceptively simple to make and has a rich and complex flavor sure to impress. They can be quite messy to make, but once the bread soaks up the egg, it will help hold all of the sandwich ingredients together.

Timesaving Tip: *If you have a waffle iron or panini maker, try cooking these sandwiches on it. Simply follow the recipe directions through step 4 and then cook 4 minutes on the preheated waffle iron brushed with melted butter.*

4 EGGS
2 TABLESPOONS 2 PERCENT MILK
FRESHLY GROUND PEPPER
4 SLICES BREAD
1 TABLESPOON DIJON MUSTARD
4 SLICES SMOKED DELI TURKEY OR HAM
2 SLICES SWISS CHEESE
OLIVE OIL COOKING SPRAY

1. In a small bowl, whisk together the eggs, milk, and pepper until thoroughly combined; set aside.

2. Place 2 slices of the bread on a clean work surface and spread 1 side evenly with the Dijon mustard.

3. Top each with 2 slices of turkey, 1 slice of cheese, and remaining slice of bread.

4. Dredge each sandwich in the egg mixture, covering completely to coat well.

5. In a large nonstick skillet coated with cooking spray over medium heat, add the sandwiches and cook until the bread is golden brown and the cheese melts, about 2 minutes on each side.

6. Serve immediately.

Tuna Niçoise Buns

MAKES 4 SERVINGS

Prep time: 15 minutes

Tuna and egg are a fabulous combination for a double dose of healthy protein. This sandwich, with its gourmet appearance, is a showstopper despite its humble ingredients. A spinoff of the popular Niçoise salad found in many restaurants in France, this sandwich includes all of those traditional ingredients: tuna, eggs, tomatoes, plump olives, and lettuce.

ONE 8-OUNCE CAN WATER-PACKED TUNA, DRAINED
1 SMALL RED ONION, THINLY SLICED
2 TABLESPOONS RED WINE VINEGAR
1 TABLESPOON FRESHLY SQUEEZED LEMON JUICE
1 TABLESPOON OLIVE OIL
SEA SALT AND FRESHLY GROUND PEPPER
2 CUPS SHREDDED LETTUCE
4 KAISER ROLLS, HALVED
1 CUP NIÇOISE OLIVES, PITTED
8 HARD-BOILED EGGS (PAGE 35), PEELED AND SLICED

1. In a large bowl, combine the tuna, onion, vinegar, lemon juice, and olive oil.

2. Season with salt and pepper.

3. Divide shredded lettuce evenly among the bottom halves of the buns and top evenly with the tuna mixture and the olives.

4. Top with the egg slices and bun tops.

5. Serve immediately.

Pesto Croque Madame

MAKES 4 SERVINGS

Prep time: 5 minutes
Cook time: 10 minutes

This twist on the traditional French sandwich has a similar taste, without the ham and béchamel sauce. Add ham or smoked turkey to the sandwich to make it more authentic, if you'd like, but try the original first before experimenting. You might find it perfect as is.

Chef's Tip: *Instead of sun-dried tomato pesto you can layer oil-packed sun-dried tomatoes on this sandwich for a more substantial lunch. The oil-packed tomatoes have a richer taste than those that need to be plumped up with water.*

2 CRUSTY KAISER ROLLS, HALVED
2 TABLESPOONS SUN-DRIED TOMATO PESTO
8 EGGS
1 TEASPOON CHOPPED FRESH PARSLEY
DASH OF HOT SAUCE
PINCH OF FRESHLY GROUND PEPPER
OLIVE OIL COOKING SPRAY
FOUR ¼-INCH-THICK SLICES SWISS OR GRUYÈRE CHEESE

1. Preheat the broiler to high.

2. Broil the Kaiser rolls 30 seconds to 1 minute, until they are toasted.

3. Spread the pesto on the cut sides of rolls.

4. Place the rolls on an aluminum foil–covered baking sheet and set aside.

5. In a medium bowl, whisk together the eggs, parsley, hot sauce, and pepper; set aside.

6. In a large skillet coated with cooking spray over medium-high heat, add the egg mixture and cook about 3 minutes, or until the eggs are set.

7. Remove the eggs from the skillet and cut into 4 pieces. Place each piece on the cut sides of the rolls.

8. Top the eggs with the cheese and broil until the cheese is melted.

Fried Egg and Bacon Tarts

MAKES 9 SERVINGS

Prep time: 15 minutes (plus freezing time)
Cook time: 20 minutes

This is a simple but decadent dish that is equally perfect for a fancy brunch or a casual family breakfast. You can actually cook the bacon right on top of the puff pastry if you don't mind cracking your eggs on top and not being able to see the bacon. You can also dress this recipe up with sautéed mushrooms, green onions, fresh herbs, and a spoon of hot salsa, depending on your taste.

1 TABLESPOON ALL-PURPOSE FLOUR, FOR ROLLING
1 FROZEN PUFF PASTRY SHEET, THAWED
11 LARGE EGGS
1 TEASPOON WATER
9 THICK-CUT BACON SLICES, COOKED AND CUT IN HALF
9 TO 18 CHERRY TOMATOES
SEA SALT AND FRESHLY GROUND BLACK PEPPER
PINCH OF RED CHILI FLAKES

1. Line a large baking sheet with parchment paper and set aside.

2. Lightly flour a clean work surface and unfold the puff pastry. Lightly flour the top of the puff pastry and roll it out evenly to a 12-inch square.

3. Cut the square into nine 4-by-4-inch squares and transfer them to the prepared baking sheet. Use a fork to prick the squares all over and place the baking tray in the freezer until the puff pastry is firm, about 30 minutes.

4. Preheat the oven to 425°F.

5. In a small bowl whisk together 2 eggs with the water. Take the puff pastry out of the freezer and lightly brush each square with the egg-water mixture.

6. Bake the pastry until it is light golden and puffed, about 15 minutes.

7. Take the baking sheet out of the oven and press the center of each square to create a shallow depression. Crack 1 egg into each square. Top each square with 2 half pieces of bacon and 1 or 2 cherry tomatoes.

8. Lightly season each square with salt and pepper. Bake the tarts an additional 5 minutes or until the eggs are set.

9. Sprinkle the tarts with red chili flakes and serve.

CHAPTER FOURTEEN

Desserts

Key Lime Pie

Prep time: 15 minutes
Cook time: 15 minutes

Key limes are smaller and sweeter than Persian limes, so try to get them for this recipe when you see the pretty mesh bags in the supermarket. Look for limes that are yellow in color indicating ripeness. While the emerald green limes tend to be prettier, they are more immature and can have a bitter, sharp flavor.

3 EGG YOLKS
2 TABLESPOONS LIME ZEST
ONE 14-OUNCE CAN SWEETENED CONDENSED MILK
½ CUP FRESHLY SQUEEZED LIME JUICE
ONE 9-INCH PREPARED GRAHAM CRACKER CRUST
1 CUP WHIPPING CREAM
4 TEASPOONS SUGAR

1. Preheat the oven to 350°F.

2. In a medium bowl, whisk together the egg yolks and lime zest until thoroughly combined. Whisk in the condensed milk and lime juice.

3. Let the filling stand for about 5 minutes.

4. Pour the filling into the crust.

5. Bake the pie for about 15 minutes or until the filling is set.

6. Remove the pie from the oven and cool for 15 minutes.

7. Cover and refrigerate the pie for at least 3 hours.

8. Beat the whipping cream and sugar until stiff peaks form.

9. Spread the whipped cream over the chilled pie.

Chocolate Soufflé

MAKES 4 SERVINGS

Prep time: 20 minutes
Cook time: 40 minutes

Is there anything as lovely and fragrant as a perfect chocolate soufflé fresh from the oven? Restaurants have built their reputations on being able to produce this masterpiece, and you can make it at home with a good set of hand beaters and some patience. Soufflés are not hard to make—they just require getting as much volume out of the beaten egg whites as possible and gentle folding to retain the airy texture.

½ CUP SUGAR

½ CUP UNSWEETENED COCOA POWDER

¼ CUP ALL-PURPOSE FLOUR

PINCH OF SEA SALT

1 CUP 2 PERCENT MILK

1 TEASPOON VANILLA EXTRACT

4 EGGS, SEPARATED AND AT ROOM TEMPERATURE

½ TEASPOON CREAM OF TARTAR

1. Preheat the oven to 350°F.

2. In a medium saucepan, whisk together ¼ cup of the sugar, cocoa, flour, salt, and milk until thoroughly combined.

3. Place the saucepan over medium heat and heat until the mixture boils and thickens, whisking constantly.

4. Whisk in the vanilla and remove the saucepan from the heat.

5. In a large stainless steel bowl, beat the egg whites and cream of tartar until foamy. Gradually add the remaining ¼ cup sugar, 2 tablespoons at a time, beating until the sugar is dissolved and glossy and stiff peaks form.

6. Whisk the egg yolks into the chocolate mixture.

7. Gently fold the chocolate mixture into the egg whites just until the mixture is combined and there are no streaks of white. Spoon the mixture into an ungreased 2-quart soufflé dish.

8. Bake the soufflé for about 30 minutes or until it is puffed and browned.

9. Serve immediately.

Apple Raisin Bread Pudding

MAKES 8 SERVINGS

Prep time: 15 minutes
Cook time: 45 minutes

Apples are a wonderful versatile ingredient and are also a healthy part of any diet. They can reduce the risk of cancer, diabetes, hypertension, and heart disease. Apples are also a wonderful source of fiber, phytonutrients, vitamin C, vitamin B$_6$, and calcium.

2 TABLESPOONS BUTTER PLUS EXTRA FOR GREASING
2 MEDIUM APPLES, PEELED, CORED AND DICED
6 SLICES BREAD, CUBED
½ CUP RAISINS
4 EGGS
2 CUPS WHOLE MILK
½ CUP FIRMLY PACKED BROWN SUGAR
1 TABLESPOON VANILLA EXTRACT
1 TEASPOON GROUND CINNAMON
PINCH OF GROUND NUTMEG

1. Preheat the oven to 350°F.

2. Use some of the butter to grease a 2-quart baking dish; set aside.

3. In a medium skillet, melt the remaining 2 tablespoons butter and cook the apples until they are softened, about 5 minutes.

4. Remove the skillet from the heat.

5. Combine the bread cubes, raisins, and cooked apples in the prepared baking dish, and toss well to blend.

6. In a medium bowl, whisk together the eggs, milk, brown sugar, vanilla, cinnamon, and nutmeg until thoroughly combined.

7. Pour the egg mixture over the bread mixture and let stand at room temperature for at least 30 minutes to allow the bread to soak up the egg mixture.

8. Bake the bread pudding for about 45 minutes or until a knife inserted near the center comes out clean.

9. Serve warm.

Double Chocolate Bread Pudding

Prep time: 30 minutes
Cook time: 60 minutes

Chocolate is an obsession for many and thankfully it's shown to have many healthy benefits due to the anti-oxidants it contains. While this custard-drenched dessert is certainly not the healthiest, try a second helping for extra antioxidants!

14 CUPS ¾-INCH CUBES FRENCH BREAD WITH CRUST (ABOUT 12 OUNCES)
6 OUNCES BITTERSWEET CHOCOLATE, CHOPPED
6 OUNCES WHITE CHOCOLATE, CHOPPED
4 EGGS
½ CUP SUGAR, DIVIDED
1 TABLESPOON VANILLA EXTRACT
2 CUPS WHIPPING CREAM
½ CUP WHOLE MILK
VEGETABLE OIL COOKING SPRAY

1. In a large bowl, combine the bread, bittersweet chocolate, and white chocolate, tossing well to blend.

2. Using an electric mixer, in a separate large bowl, beat the eggs, 6 tablespoons sugar, and vanilla until blended.

3. Gradually add 1½ cups of the whipping cream and milk, beating well.

4. Add the cream mixture to the bread mixture. Toss well to combine.

5. Let the mixture stand at room temperature for 30 minutes to allow the bread to soak up the liquid.

6. Preheat the oven to 350°F.

7. Coat a 9-by-13-inch glass baking dish with cooking spray.

8. Transfer the bread mixture to prepared dish, spreading evenly.

9. Drizzle the remaining ½ cup of whipping cream over the bread mixture.

10. Sprinkle the bread mixture with the remaining 2 tablespoons of sugar.

11. Bake the bread pudding until the edges are golden and the custard is set in the center, about 1 hour.

12. Cool the bread pudding slightly and serve warm.

Ginger and Vanilla Bean Pots de Crème

MAKES 6 SERVINGS

Prep time: 15 minutes
Cook time: 30 minutes

Ginger is an interesting ingredient that looks more like someone's gardening homework than a tasty addition to recipes. It is the underground rhizome (root) of the ginger plant and is lovely when combined with vanilla bean and cream. This dessert is rich without being too heavy and is especially perfect after a substantial entrée. The clean flavors cleanse the palate.

. . . .

Chef's Tip: *To boost the vanilla flavor even more in these pots de crème, use vanilla sugar that you have made in advance. Place a halved vanilla bean in a sealed container with sugar and let it stand for a few days, shaking it twice a day. The sugar will be infused with the vanilla and ready for the recipe.*

. . . .

2 CUPS WHIPPING CREAM
½ CUP SUGAR
2 TABLESPOONS GRATED FRESH GINGER
1 VANILLA BEAN, SPLIT LENGTHWISE
6 EGG YOLKS

1. Preheat the oven to 325°F.

2. Place six 6-ounce ramekins in a large baking pan.

3. In a medium saucepan, whisk together the cream, sugar, and ginger.

4. With a paring knife, scrape the seeds from the vanilla bean and add both the seeds and the bean to the saucepan.

5. Cook the cream mixture over medium heat, whisking constantly, until the sugar dissolves and the mixture comes to a simmer.

6. Reduce the heat to low and simmer 10 minutes. Strain the mixture through a wire-mesh strainer into a large measuring cup.

7. In a medium bowl, whisk the egg yolks until blended.

8. Gradually whisk the hot cream mixture into the yolks until just blended.

9. Return the custard mixture to the measuring cup and pour the mixture evenly into the ramekins.

10. Pour enough hot water into the baking pan to come halfway up the sides of the ramekins.

11. Bake the custards until almost set in the center when the ramekins are gently tapped, about 30 minutes.

12. Remove the custards from the water bath and cool 30 minutes.

13. Chill the custards at least 3 hours and up to 2 days.

Chocolate Pots de Crème

MAKES 6 SERVINGS

Prep time: 15 minutes
Cook time: 30 minutes

These little chocolate puddings are some of creamiest most decadent imaginable and are best enjoyed completely chilled the next day. For ease of preparation and to avoid messes, transfer the custard mixture to a large measuring cup with a pouring spout to easily pour into the ramekins. Top these mini desserts with freshly whipped cream and a few ripe raspberries for a pretty presentation.

2 CUPS HALF-AND-HALF
6 OUNCES GOOD QUALITY SEMI-SWEET CHOCOLATE, FINELY CHOPPED
1 TEASPOON VANILLA EXTRACT
6 EGG YOLKS, AT ROOM TEMPERATURE
¼ CUP SUGAR
PINCH OF SEA SALT

1. Preheat the oven to 350°F.

2. Use the butter to grease six 6-ounce ramekins. Place the ramekins in a baking pan.

3. In a medium saucepan over medium-high heat, heat the half-and-half until bubbles form around the edges. Do not boil.

4. Remove the pan from the heat and whisk in the chocolate and vanilla, stirring until very smooth.

5. Cool the chocolate mixture for about 10 minutes.

6. In a medium bowl, whisk together the egg yolks, sugar, and salt until thoroughly combined.

7. While whisking constantly, add the chocolate mixture in a slow, steady stream, stirring until blended.

8. Pour the mixture evenly into the ramekins.

9. Pour hot water into the baking pan so that the water reaches about halfway up the sides of the ramekins.

10. Bake the custards for about 30 minutes or until a knife inserted in the center comes out clean.

11. Remove the custards from the oven and from the water bath. Cool on a wire rack for at least 15 minutes. Refrigerate the custards about 3 hours or until cold.

Lemon Crème Brûlée

MAKES 6 SERVINGS

Prep time: 15 minutes
Cook time: 30 minutes

At first glance, this recipe can seem complicated, with its strainers and blowtorches, but it is really just a tart and creamy custard underneath a crisp caramel crust. While a kitchen blowtorch isn't required to make the sugary top, it is certainly fun and pretty easy to use. Find these handy gadgets at your local kitchen store.

3 CUPS HEAVY CREAM
2 TABLESPOONS LEMON ZEST
9 TABLESPOONS TURBINADO SUGAR
PINCH OF SALT
6 EGG YOLKS
1 TEASPOON VANILLA EXTRACT
1 TEASPOON FRESHLY SQUEEZED LEMON JUICE

1. Preheat the oven to 325°F and place the oven rack in the middle position.

2. Place six 6-ounce ramekins in a baking pan and set aside.

3. In a large saucepan, combine the cream and lemon zest.

4. Add 7 tablespoons of the turbinado sugar and the salt, whisking to combine.

5. Heat the mixture over medium-low heat, stirring occasionally, until bubbles form around the edges. Do not boil. Remove the pan from the heat.

6. In a medium bowl, lightly beat the the yolks.

7. While whisking constantly, gradually add the hot cream to the egg yolks in a slow, steady stream.

8. Pour the custard through a fine wire-mesh strainer into a 1-quart glass measuring cup.

9. Stir in the vanilla extract and the lemon juice.

10. Pour the mixture evenly into the ramekins.

continued ▶

11. Pour hot water into the baking pan until it comes up about halfway up the sides of the ramekins.

12. Bake the custards for 30 minutes or until they are just set around the edges but the centers wobble when the pan is gently tapped.

13. Cool the custards in the water bath for about 20 minutes. Remove the custards from the pan and refrigerate, uncovered, at least 4 hours. (Custards will set completely as they chill.)

14. Preheat the broiler to high.

15. Sprinkle about 1 teaspoon of turbinado sugar evenly over each custard. Broil the custards 1 minute or until the sugar is caramelized. Or, if using a kitchen torch, move the flame evenly back and forth close to the sugar and heat until the sugar is caramelized.

16. Let the custards stand until the caramel is hardened, about 3 to 5 minutes.

Vanilla Bean Pudding

MAKES 4 SERVINGS

Prep time: 5 minutes
Cook time: 15 minutes

Pure vanilla extract is a great choice for any dessert recipe, but for a true infusion of this popular flavor, a vanilla bean is best. It is no wonder these shiny, plump pods are so fragrant because they are the fruit (or pod) of a climbing orchid. Vanilla beans contain trace minerals and a small amount of vitamins, but they are really coveted for the flavor they impart rather than their health benefits.

. . . .

Chef's Tip: *When purchasing vanilla beans try to buy ones from Madagascar and look for pods that are slightly oily, plump, not dried up, and a shiny dark brown or black. Wrap your vanilla beans in airtight plastic and place in a cool dark area. Never store in the fridge because that can create mold on the bean.*

. . . .

3 CUPS WHOLE MILK
½ VANILLA BEAN
½ CUP SUGAR
¼ CUP CORNSTARCH
PINCH OF SEA SALT
4 EGG YOLKS
2 TABLESPOONS BUTTER

1. In a small saucepan, add the milk. Using a paring knife, scrape the seeds from the vanilla bean into the milk. Add the vanilla bean.

2. Heat the milk over low heat until the milk is hot, about 10 minutes. Remove the vanilla bean.

3. In a medium saucepan, whisk together the sugar, cornstarch, salt, and egg yolks to form a thick paste.

4. While whisking constantly, slowly add the milk mixture to the egg yolk mixture in a slow, steady stream, whisking until blended well.

5. Place the saucepan over medium heat and cook, whisking constantly until the mixture is very thick and smooth.

6. Remove the pan from the heat and whisk in the butter.

7. Spoon the pudding into serving dishes and serve warm or refrigerate for about 3 hours and serve chilled.

Pastry Cream with Fresh Berries

MAKES 4 SERVINGS

Prep time: 10 minutes
Cook time: 20 minutes

Mastering pastry cream is a great ambition because the sweet sauce is incredibly versatile and can be used for many different desserts. The trick to perfect pastry cream is to be patient and not to rush the thickening process. Avoid boiling the custard because the eggs can curdle and the milk can scorch for unfavorable results. To cool the pastry cream quickly, set the bowl of the finished sauce in an ice bath to and stir until cool.

3 LARGE EGG YOLKS
3 CUPS 2 PERCENT MILK
½ CUP SUGAR
½ CUP CORNSTARCH
PINCH OF SEA SALT
1 TEASPOON VANILLA EXTRACT
4 CUPS FRESH BERRIES

1. In a medium bowl, beat the egg yolks and milk until thoroughly combined.

2. In a large saucepan, whisk the sugar, cornstarch, and salt. Gradually whisk in the milk mixture.

3. Place the saucepan over medium-low heat and cook, whisking constantly, until the mixture just comes to a boil and thickens, about 20 minutes.

4. Boil for 1 more minute and remove the pan from the heat.

5. Stir in the vanilla extract and transfer the pastry cream to a medium bowl.

6. Cover the surface of the pastry cream with plastic wrap to prevent a skin from forming and refrigerated until completely cooled, at least 2 hours.

7. Serve the pastry cream with fresh berries.

Classic Meringues

MAKES 30 COOKIES

Prep time: 15 minutes
Cook time: 45 minutes

The trick to meringues is to dry them out slowly at a low temperature, and leaving them in the oven overnight after the oven is turned off accomplishes the desired effect. Ordinary cookies can be ruined when left exposed to air, but meringues cannot be wrecked with this type of neglect. For a real treat, dip one-half of your meringue cookies in melted chocolate or fold grated coconut into the batter.

Chef's Tip: *A pretty presentation can be achieved by spooning the cookie batter into a piping bag fitted with a large star tip to pipe perfect rosettes onto the baking sheets. You can also tint the meringues with gel food coloring paste for rainbow-colored cookies.*

6 EGG WHITES, AT ROOM TEMPERATURE
¼ TEASPOON CREAM OF TARTAR
1½ CUPS SUGAR

1. Preheat the oven to 250°F.

2. Line 2 baking sheets with parchment paper or aluminum foil and set aside.

3. In a large stainless steel bowl, beat the egg whites with a handheld electric mixer until they are frothy. Add the cream of tartar and beat until soft peaks form.

4. Add in the sugar, 1 tablespoon at a time, and beat until the sugar is dissolved and stiff glossy peaks form.

5. Dollop tablespoonfuls of batter onto the baking sheets, placing 1 inch apart.

6. Bake the meringues until firm, about 45 minutes.

7. Turn off the oven and prop the door open.

8. Leavethe meringues in the oven and cool for at least 1 hour.

9. Store the meringues in an airtight container for up to 1 week.

CHAPTER FIFTEEN

Beverages

Classic Eggnog

Prep time: 10 minutes
Cook time: 15 minutes

Eggnog is not just for the holidays, although it is traditionally served around Christmas time. It is often an alcoholic drink, so if you want to use this simple recipe as a base for cocktails, be sure it is chilled completely for the perfect amount of thickness. Adding rum or any other spirit will thin the beverage.

6 EGGS
⅓ CUP SUGAR
PINCH OF SEA SALT
4 CUPS 2 PERCENT MILK
1 TABLESPOON VANILLA EXTRACT

1. In a large saucepan, whisk together the eggs, sugar, salt, and 2 cups of the milk until thoroughly combined.

2. Place the saucepan over medium heat and cook, stirring constantly, until the mixture coats the back of a wooden spoon, about 15 minutes.

3. Remove the pan from the heat and whisk in the remaining milk.

4. Whisk in the vanilla and pour the mixture through a fine wire-mesh strainer into an airtight container.

5. Seal and refrigerate overnight.

6. Serve chilled. Store any leftovers in the refrigerator for up to 4 days.

Caramel Eggnog

MAKES 8 SERVINGS

Prep time: 10 minutes
Cook time: 20 minutes

This beverage takes a bit of skill in the kitchen because it requires making caramel from scratch and then whisking in hot water. If the water is not hot enough, the caramel can seize and become unusable. For a thicker version, substitute half-and-half or heavy cream for the milk.

· ·

Chef's Tip: *If you really don't want to attempt to make caramel, you can also substitute thick caramel sauce in this recipe for a very similar taste. Add about ¾ cup caramel to the egg and milk mixture in the recipe and continue with the steps.*

· ·

1 CUP SUGAR
6 TABLESPOONS HOT WATER
6 EGGS
4 CUPS 2 PERCENT MILK
1 TEASPOON VANILLA EXTRACT
¼ TEASPOON GROUND CINNAMON
PINCH OF SEA SALT

1. In a medium saucepan over medium-high heat, combine the sugar and 2 tablespoons of the hot water and bring the mixture to a boil.

2. Boil, without stirring, until the mixture turns a dark amber color, about 3 to 5 minutes.

3. Remove the pan from the heat and let stand for 2 minutes.

4. Carefully whisk in the remaining water and stir until well blended.

5. In a large bowl, whisk together the eggs and milk.

continued ▶

6. While whisking constantly, slowly add the caramel mixture to the milk mixture, whisking until combined. Transfer the mixture back to the saucepan.

7. Return the saucepan to medium-low heat and simmer, stirring frequently, until the mixture thickens and coats the back of a wooden spoon, about 10 minutes.

8. Strain the mixture through a fine wire-mesh strainer into a large bowl or serving pitcher.

9. Whisk in the vanilla extract, cinnamon, and salt.

10. Cover and refrigerate for about 3 hours or until completely chilled. Serve cold.

11. Refrigerate any leftovers for up to 2 days.

Protein-Packed Blueberry Smoothie

MAKES 2 SERVINGS

Prep time: 5 minutes

Anyone who has ever witnessed a bodybuilder friend slurp up whole raw eggs to meet his protein needs will certainly enjoy this delicious smoothie instead. This smoothie is packed with protein, antioxidants, and calcium, which can all contribute to good health by boosting the metabolism, improving digestion, and increasing cognitive function.

1 CUP FRESH BLUEBERRIES
1 CUP FAT-FREE GREEK YOGURT
½ CUP PASTEURIZED EGG WHITES (4 EGGS)
½ CUP RICE OR ALMOND MILK
1 TEASPOON GRATED FRESH GINGER
PINCH OF GROUND NUTMEG

1. Combine all of the ingredients in a blender.

2. Blend until smooth.

3. Serve immediately.

Cinnamon Apple Smoothie

MAKES 2 SERVINGS

Prep time: 5 minutes

This smoothie is like apple pie in a glass. What a perfect way to start the day or get an energy boost mid-afternoon! Use very fresh egg whites in this smoothie if you can't find a pasteurized egg product. Most grocery stores and health food stores do carry pasteurized eggs for recipes like this tasty smoothie.

Timesaving Tip: *You can use unsweetened applesauce instead of a fresh apple in this smoothie. Use about 1½ cups of applesauce to replace the apple or even a little more for a stronger apple flavor.*

1 LARGE TART APPLE, PEELED, CORED AND ROUGHLY CHOPPED
¼ CUP PASTEURIZED EGG WHITES (2 EGGS)
1 CUP 2 PERCENT MILK
1 TEASPOON VANILLA EXTRACT
¼ TEASPOON GROUND CINNAMON

1. Combine all of the ingredients in a blender.

2. Blend until very smooth.

3. Serve immediately.

Mango-Pear Protein Smoothie

MAKES 2 SERVINGS

Prep time: 5 minutes

This is a sweet smoothie that could pass as a dessert instead of a healthy addition to your diet. Mangoes have a unique, almost piney taste and are packed with fiber and antioxidants, including vitamin A and vitamin C. Mangoes promote healthy eyes, lower cholesterol, and can reduce the risk of cancer.

. . . .

Timesaving Tip: *Instead of a fresh mango use a good quality frozen or canned product. Get a mango product that is packed in juice rather than unhealthy sugar syrup.*

. . . .

2 FRESH, RIPE MANGOES, PEELED, PITTED, AND CUT INTO CHUNKS

1 LARGE RIPE PEAR, CORED AND CUT INTO CHUNKS

½ CUP PASTEURIZED EGG WHITES (4 EGGS)

1 CUP VANILLA-FLAVORED RICE MILK

PINCH OF GROUND NUTMEG

1. Combine all of the ingredients in a blender.

2. Blend until smooth.

3. Serve immediately.

Know Your Chicken Breeds

If you are considering raising chickens, there are many factors to consider, one of them being the type of chicken breed you will choose to raise. Before you begin to think about collecting eggs, you must first collect information on each breed. This quick-reference guide will help you get started with your research.

Chicken Breed	Personality	Egg Laying	Egg Color	Cold Hardy
Amber Star Hybrid	Sweet/friendly	Very Good (4 per week)	Brown	Yes
Ameraucana	Fun/friendly	Good (3 per week)	Light Blue	Yes
Ancona	Nervous/flighty	Excellent (5 per week)	White	Yes
Andalusian	Active/nervous	Good (3 per week)	White	No
Antwerp Belgian Bantam	Sweet/docile	Fair (2 per week)	Cream	No
Appenzeller Spitzhauben	Active/broody	Good (3 per week)	White	Yes
Araucana	Friendly	Good (3 per week)	Light Blue	Yes
Aseel	Docile/broody	Poor (1 per week)	Cream	Yes
Australorp	Quiet/docile	Excellent (5 per week)	Brown	Yes
Barnevelder	Calm/docile	Good (3 per week)	Brown	Yes
Belgian Bearded d'Uccle Bantam	Calm/friendly	Fair (2 per week)	Cream	No
Booted Bantam	Calm/broody	Fair (2 per week)	Cream	No

Chicken Breed	Personality	Egg Laying	Color	Cold Hardy
Brahma	Gentle/friendly	Good (3 per week)	Brown	Yes
Buckeye	Curious/calm	Good (3 per week)	Brown	Yes
Campine	Lively/curious	Good (3 per week)	White	Yes
Catalana	Active/unfriendly	Very Good (4 per week)	Cream	No
Chantecler	Calm/docile	Very Good (4 per week)	Brown	Yes
Cochin	Sweet/calm	Fair (2 per week)	Brown	Yes
Cornish	Docile/noisy	Poor (1 per week)	Light Brown	Yes
Crevecoeur	Aggressive/active	Fair (2 per week)	White	No
Cubalaya	Aggressive/noisy	Very Good (4 per week)	Cream	Yes
Delaware	Docile/friendly	Very Good (4 per week)	Brown	Yes
Dominique	Calm/broody	Good (3 per week)	Brown	Yes
Dorking	Friendly/calm	Good (3 per week)	Cream	Yes
Dutch	Active/lively	Fair (2 per week)	Cream	Yes
Easter Eggers	Docile/friendly	Very Good (4 per week)	Green/Blue/Pink	Yes
Faverolles	Docile/sweet	Very Good (4 per week)	Light Brown	Yes
Fayoumi	Lively/slightly wild	Fair (2 per week)	Cream	No
Hamburg	Active/unfriendly	Very Good (4 per week)	White	Yes
Holland	Friendly/calm	Good (3 per week)	White	Yes
Houdan	Docile/friendly	Fair (2 per week)	White	No

Chicken Breed	Personality	Egg Laying	Color	Cold Hardy
Jaerhon	Active/flighty	Very Good (4 per week)	White	Yes
Japanese Bantam	Docile/broody	Poor (1 per week)	Cream	No
Java	Calm/friendly	Good (3 per week)	Brown	Yes
Jersey Giant	Gentle/friendly	Good (3 per week)	Brown	Yes
La Fleche	Flighty/unfriendly	Good (3 per week)	White	No
Lakenvelder	Flighty/unfriendly	Good (3 per week)	Cream	No
Langshan	Active/friendly	Good (3 per week)	Brown	Yes
Leghorn (Nonwhite)	Nervous/noisy	Good (3 per week)	White	No
Leghorn (White)	Curious/noisy	Very Good (4 per week)	White	Yes
Malay	Aggressive/active	Poor (1 per week)	Light Brown	No
Marans	Broody/active	Good (3 per week)	Chocolate	Yes
Minorca	Active/unfriendly	Very Good (4 per week)	White	No
Modern Game	Aggressive/active	Poor (1 per week)	White	No
Naked Neck (Turken)	Docile/calm	Fair (2 per week)	Light Brown	Yes
New Hampshire Red	Aggressive/curious	Good (3 per week)	Brown	Yes
Old English Game	Aggressive/noisy	Fair (2 per week)	Cream	Yes
Orpington	Docile/friendly	Good (3 per week)	Brown	Yes
Penedesenca	Active/unfriendly	Good (3 per week)	Chocolate	No
Phoenix	Docile/broody	Poor (1 per week)	Cream	No

Chicken Breed	Personality	Egg Laying	Color	Cold Hardy
Plymouth Rock	Bossy/friendly	Very Good (4 per week)	Brown	Yes
Polish	Calm/docile	Fair (2 per week)	White	No
Redcap	Active	Good (3 per week)	White	Yes
Rhode Island	Easygoing	Excellent (5 per week)	Brown	Yes
Rosecomb Bantam	Docile/friendly	Poor (1 per week)	Cream	Yes
Russian Orloff	Calm/unfriendly	Fair (2 per week)	Light Brown	Yes
Sebright Bantam	Sprightly/curious	Poor (1 per week)	Cream	No
Sicilian Buttercup	Active/flighty	Fair (2 per week)	White	No
Silkie Bantam	Sweet/broody	Good (3 per week)	Cream	Yes
Star	Sweet/docile	Excellent (5 per week)	Brown	Yes
Sultan	Calm/friendly	Poor (1 per week)	White	No
Sumatra	Active/broody	Poor (1 per week)	White	Yes
Sussex	Curious/gentle	Very Good (4 per week)	Light Brown	Yes
Welsummer	Lively/docile	Very Good (4 per week)	Chocolate	Yes
White-Faced Black Spanish	Noisy/unfriendly	Good (3 per week)	White	No
Wyandotte	Easygoing	Very Good (4 per week)	Brown	Yes
Yokohama	Docile/broody	Poor (1 per week)	Cream	No

Egg Feedback Chart

Use this section as a guide to track all the different type of eggs you've prepared. Record what you liked and did not like, and use your notes as a reference when it's time to go shopping for eggs.

TYPE OF EGG	USE AGAIN?	COST	RECIPES MADE	NOTES
Cage-Free Eggs				
Store-Bought Conventional Eggs				
Fertile Eggs				
Free-Range Eggs				
Omega-3-Enriched Eggs				

TYPE OF EGG	USE AGAIN?	COST	RECIPES MADE	NOTES
Organic Eggs				
Pasture-Raised or Pastured Eggs				
Store-Bought Conventional Eggs				
Vegetarian-Fed Eggs				

Resources for Raising Chickens

BOOKS + PERIODICALS

ABC of Poultry Raising: A Complete Guide for the Beginner or Expert by J. H. Florea

A Guide To Better Hatching by Janet Stromberg

Backyard Poultry Magazine

Chick Days: An Absolute Beginner's Guide to Raising Chickens from Hatching to Laying by Jenna Woginrich

Chickens In Your Backyard: A Beginner's Guide by Rick Luttmann

Chickens: Tending A Small-Scale Flock For Pleasure And Profit (Hobby Farms) by Sue Weaver

Choosing and Keeping Chickens by Chris Graham

Family Poultry Flock by H. Lee Schwanz

Garden Poultry Keeping by J. Barnes

Hens in the Garden, Eggs in the Kitchen by Charlotte Popescu

Incubation at Home (Gold Cockerel) by Michael Roberts

Keep Chickens! Tending Small Flocks in Cities, Suburbs, and Other Small Spaces by Barbara Kilarski

Keeping Pet Chickens: You Don't Need Much Space to Enjoy the Bounty of Fresh Eggs from Your Own Small Flock of Happy Hens by Johannes Paul

Living with Chickens: Everything You Need to Know to Raise Your Own Backyard Flock by Geoff Hansen

Modern Free Range: For the Smaller Farmer (Gold Cockerel Series) by Michael Roberts

Poultry for Anyone by Victoria Roberts

Poultry House Construction (Gold Cockerel) by Michael Roberts

Raising Chickens For Dummies by Kimberly Willis and Rob Ludlow

Raising Poultry Successfully by Will Graves

Rare Poultry Breeds by David Scrivener

Storey's Guide to Raising Chickens: Care/Feeding/Facilities by Gail Damerow

Storey's Guide to Raising Poultry: Breeds, Care, Health by Leonard S. Mercia

Storey's Illustrated Guide to Poultry Breeds by Carol Ekarius

Success with Baby Chicks: A Complete Guide to Hatchery Selection, Mail-Order Chicks, Day-Old Chick Care, Brooding, Brooder Plans, Feeding, and Housing by Robert Plamondon

The Chicken Health Handbook by Gail Damerow

The Joy of Keeping Chickens by Jennifer Megyesi

Your Chickens: A Kid's Guide to Raising and Showing by Gail Damerow

WEBSITES + BLOGS

Art of Manliness // www.artofmanliness.com/2013/03/26/how-to-raise-backyard-chickens

Backyard Chickens // www.backyardchickens.com

Backyard Chicken Keeping // www.backyardchickenkeeping.com

Chicken-Raising // www.chicken-raising.com

City Chickens // www.citychickens.com

For the Love of Chickens // www.fortheloveofchickens.com

How to Raise Chickens // http://howtoraisechickens.org

Keeping Chickens // www.keeping-chickens.com

My Pet Chicken // www.mypetchicken.com

Planet Poultry // http://planetpoultry.com.au

Poultry Keeper // http://poultrykeeper.com

Poultry One // http://poultryone.com

Raise Your Own Chickens // http://raiseyourownchickens.com

Raising-Chickens // www.raising-chickens.org

The City Chicken // www.thecitychicken.com

Urban Chickens // http://urbanchickens.org

References

Ashway, Marty. How to Raise Chickens. Accessed December 30, 2013. http://howtoraisechickens.org/.

Backyard Chickens. Accessed December 30, 2013. http://www.backyardchickens.com/.

Balch, Phyllis A. *Prescription for Nutritional Healing, Fifth Edition: A Practical A-to-Z Reference to Drug-Free Remedies Using Vitamins, Minerals, Herbs & Food Supplements*. 5th ed. New York, NY: Avery Trade, 2010.

"Chicken Breeds." Hobby Farms. Accessed January 1, 2014. http://www.hobbyfarms.com/farm-breeds /poultry_chickens_all_landing.aspx.

Colbin, Annemarie. *Food and Healing*. Toronto: Random House, 1986.

"Eggs, Pasture Raised." The World's Healthiest Foods. Accessed December 31, 2013. http://www.whfoods.com /genpage.php?tname=foodspice&dbid=92.

Haas, Elson M., and Buck Levin. *Staying Healthy with Nutrition: The Complete Guide to Diet and Nutritional Medicine*. Rev. ed. Berkley, CA: Celestial Arts, 2006.

Librairie Larousse. *Larousse Gastronomique: The World's Greatest Culinary Encyclopedia, Completely Revised and Updated*. Toronto: Random House, 2009.

Masui, Kate. "Home Fresh Eggs: How to Raise Chickens in Your Backyard." Canadian Living. Accessed January 1, 2014. http://www.canadianliving.com/life/green_living/home_fresh_eggs_how_to_raise _chickens_in_your_backyard.php.

"Salmonella." Public Health Agency of Canada. Accessed January 2, 2014. http://www.phac-aspc.gc.ca /fs-sa/fs-fi/salmonella-eng.php.

Wood, Rebecca. *The New Whole Foods Encyclopedia: A Comprehensive Resource for Healthy Eating*. Rev. ed. New York: Penguin Books, 2010.

Zelman, Kathleen M. "Good Eggs: For Nutrition, They're Hard to Beat." WebMD. Accessed January 1, 2014. http://www.webmd.com/diet/features/good-eggs-for-nutrition-theyre-hard-to-beat.

Recipe Index

Index

Made in the USA
San Bernardino, CA
01 December 2019

60690734R00122